Falling into Faith

Falling into Faith

Lectio Divina Series
Cycle C

Robert J. Miller

SHEED & WARD

Franklin, Wisconsin

As an apostolate of the Priests of the Sacred Heart, a Catholic religious congregation, the mission of Sheed & Ward is to publish books of contemporary impact and enduring merit in Catholic Christian thought and action. The books published, however, reflect the opinion of their authors and are not meant to represent the official position of the Priests of the Sacred Heart.

2000

Sheed & Ward
7373 South Lovers Lane Road
Franklin, Wisconsin 53132
1-800-266-5564

Scripture quotations are lectionary based.

Printed in the United States of America

Cover and interior design: GrafixStudio, Inc.

Library of Congress Cataloging-in-Publication Data

Miller, Robert J., priest.
    Falling into faith : lecto divina series, cycle C / Robert J. Miller.
    p.cm.
    ISBN 1-58051-078-7 (alk. paper)
    Devotional calendars—Catholic Church. 2. Bible—Meditations.
    3. Catholic Church—Prayer-books and devotions—English.
    4. Catholic Church. Lectionary for Mass (U.S.) I. Title.

BX2182.2 .M56 2000
242'.2—dc21

                                                    00-041016

1 2 3 4 5 / 03 02 01 00

FOREWORD

In this, his third book, Fr. Bob Miller stands in the spiritual/literary tradition of such luminaries as Louis Evely, Thomas Merton, Kathleen Norris, Henri Nouwen, and Basil Pennington. He provides a context in which we can explore our inner selves through the lens of sacred Scripture and shared human experience.

The practice of *lectio divina*—an introspective, prayerful reading of the biblical text—can be a particularly inviting and useful spiritual discipline for personal growth. Accessing the wisdom of divine Revelation through careful reflection is a technique as old as the Bible itself. The term *lectio* comes out of the Catholic Christian monastic tradition. The beauty of our present day is, that which has been closeted in monastic cloisters is now accessible and available to the average person in the pew. Some of the finest pieces of the rich inheritance of the monastic spiritual tradition—once perceived as exotic or beyond the ordinary Christian—are now powerful resources for every soul that chooses to encounter Christ in these ancient and hallowed ways.

Noted teacher and writer Michael Downey concretely introduces the practice of *lectio divina* by explaining that it is:

> . . . sacred reading in which reading is an act of the whole body,
> done slowly, often aloud, as if chewing over a few words so that they
> may be ingested. The book is held, sounds are taken in, becoming

part of the reader. Pages are gazed upon, fingered and felt, held, caressed. And smelled. Put simply, if it is true that "you are what you eat," the ancient practice of lectio teaches that we become what we read. In lectio we learn the words by heart. Word comes to be written into the very skin of us.

This work uniquely acknowledges the depths to which lectio invites the reader to plumb. Its organizational principle is the wisdom succinctly and profoundly contained in the Church's lectionary, and its content is drawn from the lived pastoral experience of its author. The movement toward psycho-spiritual integration, toward which all genuine spirituality points, is an intended outcome as each reflection is crafted with an eye to utilizing the soulful wisdom of depth psychology.

The words of the biblical text are described as "sweeter than honey" (see Psalm 19). The psalmist invites us to "taste and see the goodness of the Lord" (see Psalm 34). The reign of God is described as a rich banquet feast (see Matthew 22:2–14). The Scriptures and reflections contained herein are designed to spiritually sustain, nourish, and nurture the reader. There is something very good here. I invite you to enter and partake.

—Stephen J. Hrycyniak
Publisher

"Falling Into Faith"

*Pulling out the chair
Beneath your mind
And watching you fall upon God—
There is nothing else for Hafiz to do
That is more fun in this world!*

Shams-Ud-Din Mohammed Hafiz
Muslim mystic (1320–1389)

When I was a boy, I once spent a glorious afternoon leaping off the rafters of a barn into endless bales of hay. Although thrilled with the experience, I paid a price within hours when I discovered that I was allergic to hay. Hours of sneezing and congestion led me to a doctor who confirmed the diagnosis and prescribed medication.

This story is symbolic allegory for what I also learned about God and faith. Somewhere along the line, I learned it was unsafe to "fall" uncontrolled through life, and that the only way God could be experienced was through steady, unrelenting discipline. Salvation could only be earned through hard work, prayer, virtue, discipline, and strict self-control. The sacraments, the rosary, reading Scripture (that came later in life!), following one's "divine" vocation—these were the methods through which one could attain heaven and acquire a virtuous lifestyle.

Now some fifty years into life, I have slowly relearned the indescribable joy of falling uncontrolled—this time, into the arms of a God of total Grace and Gift. I have begun to learn what Gabriel Marcel said so well: "Life is not a problem to be solved, but a mystery to be lived." Faith is not so much something to be achieved or acquired by rules and regulations; rather, it is more a Grace-full mystery one cannot help but fall into and completely yield to. Faith is becoming a Spirit-seeker—becoming truly "catholic" in searching and pursuing God wherever Grace may be found.

God is a *Mystery* that one simply falls into. God's gifts cannot be earned, merited, controlled, or manipulated by prayer or action in any way. Our God is Gift.

God is a *Lover* who receives everything and forgives everything. The core of his Word is *"to give his people knowledge of salvation through forgiveness of their sins"* (Luke 1:77). Where we obsess about sin and failure, God obsesses about love and compassion!

God is a *Hound of Heaven*, an image borrowed from the poem by this name, written by Francis Thompson (1859–1907). We cannot avoid God, run away from him, or escape him! Try it by whatever means we choose (and many have tried by many means in today's world), and sooner or later, you will turn a corner and find God standing squarely in your path waiting. The true Mystery here is that God's power, forgiveness, and love will always get to you. You cannot resist it because *"Greater is he that is in you, than he that is in the world"* (1 John 4:4). God is always greater! Greater than sin, suffering, failure.

So what can we humans do in response? What should we do? Does "falling into faith" mean absolute quietism or passivity? On the contrary! The challenge of faith in the new millennium will be *awareness, surrender, and gratitude.*

1) Become *aware* of the true reality of our God—his encompassing Presence, his Passion for his people, his unceasing efforts to draw us closer to him. Know that these Truths touch the essence of God far more than our regulations, rules, and religious achievements. True awareness of the Divine is more an unlearning than a learning.

2) *Surrender* to God your bodies, souls, and spirits—and your ego-illusions of success, control, and competence. Fall into God's arms completely. Yield

up everything to this God who has "done it all" for you. Faith is a floating in the sea of Grace—and allowing Grace to flow in and through every pore of your mind, ego, body, and spirit.

3) Have a daily *attitude of gratitude.* In the end, all we humans can do is simply sit quietly before Greatness and Power. Our words fail, our actions fall short most of the time, our lives are poor attempts at modeling this Love. Thus all we do is sit and say:

> Thank you God that it does not depend on me! Thank
> you for our forgiveness in our brokenness and poverty.
> Thank you for your peace and power. Thank you that I
> am only part of the "Great River" that is your Love and
> Life. I am. You are. Life is. Grace flows. That is enough.

Finally, this message of "falling into faith" is a dangerous one. This message upsets people who have carefully constructed a "meritocracy of faith," people who have built their lives upon rigid control and personal righteousness before a Deity whose love must be earned. Perhaps this is why Jesus himself was killed: *"He stirs up the people by his teaching throughout the whole of Galilee"* (Luke 23:5).

Only a few have dared teach these truths, and we best call them "prophets" today. Certainly Jesus Christ, Julian of Norwich in the past, Richard Rohr today. Most of us have a problem with prophets (especially living ones) because they see life in a different way, and call other believers to do so as well.

May you be one of those true believers, those modern Spirit-seekers who dare to see life and faith differently—the way Jesus saw it!

—Robert Miller
November 1999

Using Lectio Divina in Your Prayer Life

This collection of lectionary-based Scripture meditations is written for a twofold purpose: to offer contemporary insights into the timeless wisdom of Scripture, and to inspire and deepen one's personal prayer and praise of our amazing God. In essence, these two purposes are what this time-honored tradition is all about.

As you commit yourself to the practice of *lectio divina*, you will want to establish a special place for your prayer time. This should be an area that is free of distractions and clutter, where you can sit comfortably and quietly for perhaps as long as thirty minutes. You will need a personal Bible (or some other source containing the full text of Scripture readings for that particular day) and any other items that help you enhance your sacred space (candles, notepad and pen, background music).

The practice of *lectio divina* consists of several simple steps. Following these steps in structuring your own meditations and Scripture study times will easily double the effectiveness and power of these times.

1. *Prepare yourself*

Mindfully enter your sacred prayer place and position yourself comfortably. As you mentally choose to clear your mind of worries, concerns, and pressures, center your thoughts and feelings upon God and his goodness to you.

2. *Read Scripture*

Open your Bible and locate the passages selected for the day. First, read the passages slowly and in their entirety, and let the message "sink into" your spirit. Then, read the passages (or parts of them) a second time, if you desire.

3. *Read the reflection*

Slowly read the reflection, pausing frequently to take in concepts. Allow them to challenge or soothe you while you pray spontaneously. This is not unlike "chewing" food; you turn words and phrases over and over in your mind as you pray and meditate on their import in your life. Allow words of prayer or praise to surface, and speak them to your God.

4. *Resolutions*

As you approach the end of your prayer time, conclude with silent resolutions or commitments of things you will attempt to do differently as a result of your meditation. Make these directly to your God. End with prayers of thanksgiving and gratitude for what God has done, is doing, and will yet do in your life. Again, completely place your life this day in God's hands.

The "Great Day"

First Sunday of Advent

(Jeremiah 33:14–16; 1 Thessalonians 3:12–4:2; Luke 21:25–36)

Everyone has anxiously awaited
    some special day to come in their life—
    a birthday, a wedding, a new job.
There is nervous tension and apprehension,
    but also excitement
        and anticipation.
God, too, has special days standing out
    from others as divine history rolls by.
"The great day will suddenly close in . . .
    the day I speak of will come upon all
    who dwell on the face of the earth,
    so be on the watch" (Luke 21:34–36).

The first "great day" was foretold
    thousands of years beforehand—
    and it fulfilled a divine promise
        of a special person,
        of a glorious freedom,
        of an other-worldly peace.
"In those days I will raise up a just shoot;
    he will do what is right and just
    in the land" (Jeremiah 33:15).

The unheralded coming of Jesus
   from simple, poor Bethlehem
   was a great day
   few were prepared for.

Yet another "great day" was promised
   by Jesus to his followers
   on the eve of his own
      "greatest day"—
   the coming of a Helper and Guide,
      a Spirit of power and peace
   who would "guide them to all truth."
Locked away from their enemies in fear,
   Jesus' followers were unprepared
      for that divine Energy
   that would transform their local sect
      into a worldwide church.
"It shall come to pass
   in the last days,
   that I will pour out
   a portion of my Spirit
      on all mankind . . . " (Acts 2:17).

There are still other "great days" coming,
   days that directly affect you,
   and that will demand a response.
One of those "great days"
   will be your last day in this world—
   a day all know is coming
   but few dare speak of,
      except in hushed and muted tones.
"Stay awake therefore! You cannot know
the day your Lord is coming" (Matthew 25:42).

In biblical times, this day was spoken of
   as a fearsome, terrible thing.
"On the earth,
   nations will be in anguish . . .

*men will die of fright
in anticipation of what
is coming on the earth"* (Luke 21:26).
Today our "educated, sophisticated" world
chuckles at this antiquated imagery—
yet dare we ignore the stark reality
and dark truth behind these words?

The day is indeed coming
when life's account books
will be balanced,
when the sum of our actions
will be added,
when we will stand before the One
"who knows how to ask questions."
*"When these things begin,
stand erect and raise your heads,
for your ransom is at hand"* (Luke 21:28).

On this, our personal "greatest day,"
an equally great decision
will be rendered—
our place and status for eternity.
What that place is,
how our status is decided
will depend upon
the number and quality
of other "great days"
in our life.

How many "great days"
were there in your life
when "you overflowed
with love for one another,"
when you "conducted yourself in a way
pleasing to your God,"
when you "made still greater progress"
in prayer, humbleness, and honesty,

when you responded to God with
  complete surrender,
  total gratitude?

"Pray constantly for the strength . . .
  to stand secure before the Son of Man" (Luke 21:36).

Miracles in the Desert

Second Sunday of Advent

(Baruch 5:1–9; Luke 3:1–6)

The Sahara Desert.
Death Valley.
The vast desert areas
    of southwestern United States:
these are truly barren places—
    wild and primitive desert places,
    with hills of sand and stone,
    with a starkly arid, waterless beauty,
    often impassible,
        mountainous,
        forbidding,

Only vague winding trails exist,
    made by desert animals
    truly at home
        in this dry wilderness.
These are not places
    where people usually choose
    to make a home.

At times our life may feel like
    a dry and barren desert.

We may face mountains of problems,
   valleys of fear or abandonment,
   impassible terrains of loss and grief,
   dry, arid periods
      of no apparent personal support,
   with wild, unknown forces looming,
      ready to pounce.

But there is a divine truth
   about life's "desert places,"
   a dark truth hard to believe:
      out of the desert comes life!
It is part of God's wisdom that
   from the dryness and aridity
      of personal deserts,
   from fear, frustration, and failure,
      can come miracles of rebirth!
"Every valley shall be filled,
   every mountain and hill leveled" (Luke 3:5).

Viewed from a spiritual framework,
   desert places may even be necessary
   for personal transformation to occur.
Some endings and deaths in life
   are needed for new life to emerge—
   after all, it was only Jesus' death
      that gave life to all.

Out of life's deserts
   can come miracles of rebirth.
This is a great spiritual truth
   because it is grounded
   not on human capability
      but divine availability.

The simple fact is, we have a God
   whose very Name is
   "Author of Life"—
   a God always present to
     and powerful for
   his beloved children.
For our God,
   miracles in the desert
     are routine—
Miracles such as Israel's
   forty years of desert wandering,
   ending in a "promised land"
   of milk and honey.
Miracles such as the Baptist
   coming from the desert
   preaching of Another to come,
   one who would bring life and salvation.

With our Creator God,
   no desert is lifeless,
   no situation hopeless.
"They had said 'Our bones are dried up,
   our hope is lost, we are cut off.'
Thus says the Lord:
   I will open your graves
   and have you rise from them.
I will put my spirit on you
   that you may live" (Ezekiel 38:12–14).

Look back at your own life
   to rediscover
     forgotten miracles.
How many times
   has your wandering turned to finding,
   your loneliness turned to love,
   your struggle turned to inner strength?

As a beloved child of God,
   you have been blessed with
   the gift of remarkable hope
   and immense personal resiliency.
You have a God who can truly
   make a way for you
   where there is no way—
   a God who can make miracles
   bloom like desert wildflowers
      in your "desert places."

Today, your God reminds you:
   "Every valley will be filled,
   every mountain will be leveled,
   the winding ways will be made straight
   and the rough ways smooth" (Luke 3:5).

Hope Will Not Be Silenced

Third Sunday of Advent

(Philippians 4:4–7; Luke 3:10–18)

It was June of 1955.
Winston Churchill
    was at the end of his life,
    but was asked to give
        a commencement talk.
He looked sick and frail,
    held onto the podium for dear life,
    and took an eternity
        before he spoke a word.
Finally, the man who had called Britain
    back from destruction
        in World War II,
    who had known great political setbacks,
        raised his head to speak.
In his last public talk,
    Churchill spoke only three sentences:
"Never give up.
    Never give up!
        NEVER give up!!"

Despite the immense burdens
   of their life,
   the truly great people
   are those who have learned
      one great lesson:
   hope can never be silenced.
For anyone who believes
   in Powers greater than self,
   Powers greater than this world,
      hope will always break out—
   for the energy of Hope
   is an irrepressible,
      undeniable force.

"In Him who is the source of my strength,
   I have strength for everything" (Philippians 4:13).
The more life presses us
   and the world stresses us,
   and the heaviest of burdens
      weighs us down,
   the more our God reminds us,
   "I will be with you always,
   even until the end of time" (Matthew 28).

Hope lies not in
   the absence of problems,
   but in the presence
   of peace within.
Having Hope does not mean
   having no problems or worries;
   rather, having Hope means
   knowing and believing
      with every fiber of our being
   that what we *have* is greater than
      what we *lack*.

"The Lord himself is near . . .
  dismiss all anxiety
  from your minds" (Philippians 4:5–6).

Leon-Joseph Suenens said it best:
  "I am a man of hope,
  not for human reasons
  nor from any natural optimism.
But because I believe the Holy Spirit
  is at work
  in the Church and
  in the world.
To those who welcome him
  he gives fresh liberty
  and renewed joy and hope.
I believe in the surprises of the Holy Spirit.
To Hope is a duty, not a luxury."

What are you worried about?
What is pulling down your spirit?
"Dismiss all anxiety from your minds."

What personal weakness
  obsesses you?
What perceived deficiency
  holds you back?
"The Lord himself is near you."

Send away your fears.
Dismiss your distress and dread.
Seek a Source of Power and Peace
  beyond this plane of existence—
    for Hope can never be silenced.

"He will baptize you
in the Holy Spirit and in fire!" (Luke 3:16)

Never give up on God!
Never give up on yourself!
Never give up!

Insignificant People

Fourth Sunday of Advent

(Micah 5:1–4; Luke 1:39–45)

As you hear retold once again
   the poignant Christmas story,
   listen carefully and look well
   at the utter absence
      of powerful people.
There are virtually no famous people,
   no one of great wealth
      or social status,
   no one of great significance or import
      in the world of that time.
Every major player in the Christmas drama
is a "small person"—
   insignificant, powerless,
      truly "ordinary."

Mary and Joseph were humble Galileans—
   so poor and without help
   they could not even rent an inn
   in which to birth their Child.

Their Newborn would grow up poor—
    they later would pay
    the lowest temple offering
    allowed by the Law.

The shepherds in the fields
    who greeted the Newborn Child
    were the despised underclass
    of Israel.
They were generally considered
    dirty, untrustworthy thieves
    by most people.

Zechariah and Elizabeth were seniors—
    a forgotten elderly couple,
    burdened with the "poverty"
    of childlessness—
considered the greatest misfortune
    for people of that time.

Even the village of Jesus' birth,
    the little town of Bethlehem,
    was a place so unimportant
    it was not even mentioned
    in the Old Testament.

The utter insignificance
    of God's specially chosen people
    is most appropriate and symbolic—
God always chooses outcasts
    to proclaim Good News.
Consistently throughout history,
    God has used the powerless
    to humble the powerful.

Moses had few if any speaking gifts.
Jeremiah was a mere youth,
    and "knew not how to speak."

The queen Esther was an adopted orphan,
    the widow Ruth abandoned country for love.
Peter was an impulsive fisherman,
    Paul a rigid legalist.
Francis was thought to be crazy,
    Ghandi a fool for his pacifism,
    Dr. King an agitator and malcontent,
    Mother Teresa an insignificant simple nun.

It is abundantly clear from history
    that God's personal preference
    is for insignificant people,
    powerless people,
    humble people.
"God has thrown down rulers from their thrones,
    but lifted up the lowly.
The hungry he has filled with good things,
    the rich he has sent away empty" (Luke 1:52–53).

The world today obsesses
    about the rich and powerful,
    about conspicuous wealth and power,
    the "promised land" of financial security,
        success, prosperity.
What a powerfully symbolic message
    our yearly Christmas story teaches—
    the One born in a stable
    fits none of these categories.
The story of the birth of Jesus sums up
    God's entire vision and plan
    for humanity—
        and for you.

Rejoice not in your greatness,
    but seek for the "smallness"
        of a humble, contrite spirit.

Do not celebrate prosperity and security,
but take joy in the "insignificance"
of simple integrity and just acts.
Never glory in personal power or control,
but rest easy in the powerlessness
of total commitment to your God.

"God rescues the poor when they cry out,
the oppressed who have no one to help.
He shows pity to the needy and the poor,
and saves the lives of the poor.
Blessed be the Lord,
who alone does wonderful deeds" (Psalm 72:13–14, 18).

Living in Darkness, Seeing the Light

Christmas

(Isaiah 9:1–6; John 1:1–18)

The story is told of a man searching for keys
   underneath a bright overhead light.
When a friend asked where the keys were lost,
   the man pointed into the shadows
   saying, "Over there in the dark."
When questioned why he didn't search there,
   the man replied,
"Because the light is better here."

Too many people prefer living
   in predictable patterns of darkness
   rather than facing the transformation
   of walking in the light
     with the Light.

For generations people have lived with
   this "life-darkness" of discouragement and despair,
   in the gloom of loneliness, grief, and fear.
But the birth of the Child-God changed all that.
*"The people who walked in darkness
   have seen a great light"* (Isaiah 9:1).

Our modern age has more darkness than ever—
　　the dim despairs of addiction, lust, and greed,
　　the shadowy shallowness of this world's values
　　　　(competition, control, individualism),
　　the dark illusions of materialist self-sufficiency.
But again, the voice of utter Simplicity
　　in the guise of a Bethlehem Baby
　　rings out a peal of hope and healing:
"I am the Light of the world!
　　No follower of mine
　　shall ever walk in darkness;
　　they shall possess the light of Life!" (John 8:12)

Yet within this Christmas story
　　of great joy for all the world,
　　there lies a hidden lesson of great wisdom
　　awaiting only those few who
　　"have eyes to see, and ears to hear."

Notice who it was that recognized and accepted
　　the Newborn "Light of the world":
　　not kings, politicians, or church leaders,
　　not successful business people, builders, or bankers,
　　not even "normal" everyday people.

It was, instead, the dispossessed and castoffs—
　　outcast shepherds, wandering wise men,
　　　　lowly animals.
It was the *anawim,* the "poor little ones"—
　　the ignored, forgotten, and overlooked ones
　　　　living in the darkness of the world,
　　poor in wealth and possessions
　　　　but rich in humbleness, honesty, and trust.

It seems those best able to receive the "Light"
    are those who are "poor in spirit"—
      those humble enough to admit their nothingness,
        wise enough to come with simplicity,
        courageous enough to surrender to God.
"How blessed are the poor in spirit,
    the reign of God is theirs" (Matthew 5:3).

Not all those who have "seen the great light"
    are willing to walk in that Light.
"To his own he came,
    yet his own did not accept him" (John 1:10–11).

In the confusing darkness of this age,
    as Bethlehem's Star shines again,
    are you humble enough to bow at the manger,
    and poor enough to give all you have
      to the Babe of Bethlehem?

Can you leave predictable patterns
    of puffed-up pride and vanity,
    obsession with image and control,
    avoiding responsibility and commitment,
    lack of time for prayer and socially just actions?

Can you truly accept the fullness
    of the radical Grace Jesus came to bring—
    no matter what changes it may make
      to your life, speech, actions, job,
      to your friends and relationships,
      to your attitudes and emotions?

Come to the Light that is Jesus.
Find healing for the darkness of this age,
    and peace for your aching soul.
"Whatever came to be in him, found life,
    life for the light of men.
The light shines on in the darkness,
    a darkness that did not overcome it" (John 1:4–5).

"In My Father's House"

Holy Family

(Colossians 3:12–21; Luke 2:41–52)

"Did you not know I had to be
in my Father's house?'
But they did not grasp
what he said to them" (Luke 2:49).
Neither does most of our world
grasp the depth in these words.

At the age of twelve, Jesus already knew
of the two conflicting worldviews
competing for our attention.
Although active in every age,
never have these forces been so
opposed as in this generation.
Jesus made his choice while still a child—
now the choice is yours.
"Choose this day who you will serve" (Joshua 24:15).

The "market-place" view of life
promotes competition and control:
economics is the game,
buying and selling is the paradigm
(and everything has a price).

Reality is based on "market value,"
    and ego-obsession predominates—
        rampant individualism,
        identity and image fixations,
        addiction, acquisition, attainment.
"What does it profit a person if
    he gains the world but loses his soul?" (Matthew 16:26)

The "Father's house" view of life
    values action rooted in contemplation;
    surrender and conversion is the pattern,
    and everything has priceless inherent value.
Reality is based on other-worldly Truths:
    personal awareness and ego-releasing dominate—
    "I am not who the world thinks I am.
    I am not even who I pretend to be.
    I am simply a child of my God.
    Life is not about me or my issues,
        but about God and our issues."
"I have come to rate all as loss
    compared with the surpassing knowledge
    of Jesus Christ" (Philippians 3:8).

When Jesus began his public ministry,
    his first words shockingly announced
    this completely uprooted world order.
"The Kingdom of God is at hand!
    Reform your lives,
        and believe the Good News!" (Mark 1:15)
What a truly radical revolution—
    a world saved through re-formed relationships,
    transformed through the utter simplicity of Love!

No longer are people entrapped
    by injustice, despair, obsession, sin—
    or with sickness, blindness, or captivity.

These consequences of market-place materialism
    are transformed by radical Grace,
        surpassed by powers of Love,
        healed by tender Mercies.
"Greater is he that is in me
    than he that is in the world" (1 John 4:4).

Although we might believe in God,
    our worldview may need radical surgery.
Swimming daily in the world's currents,
    our ego learns to control, dominate, and "fix"—
    for the illusions of comfort, image, and security.
Thus, although our prayers say one thing,
    our actions can become addictive and grasping.

Your goal should be to live in your Father's house—
    completely at rest in an utterly simple God,
    freed from compulsion, anxiety, or fear,
    acting at all times out of love,
    moving forward in grace and freedom.

Develop skills of self-reflection—
    for only in brutally honest "unlearning"
    can you unmask the illusions sold to you daily,
    the pretentious self-images you develop
        in the world's market place.
Get rid of any illusions
    so you can live in the Presence.

Learn to develop awareness—
    awareness of God's Reality,
    of your freedom in Truth,
    of Life around you,
    of a world crying for justice.

True religion is always about "seeing."
That is why Jesus and Buddha
    both say, "Stay awake!"

Be awake to the passing illusions
of our market-place world.
Come alive to the eternal Reality
of living in your Father's house.

faith Is in the Journey

Epiphany

(Matthew 2:1–12)

The cowardly lion, the scarecrow,
 the tin man, Dorothy, and Todo:
 few can forget these
  Wizard of Oz legends.
All were searching for something,
 and journeyed to someone
  who could bestow it,
 only to find their unique gifts
 not in their destination—
 but in journeying
  along the road.

Our own life in this world
 can be compared to a journey:
 there are "beginning" times
  of nervous excitement;
 "weary" times
  when the road seems long and lonely;
 all too rare, "ecstasy" times
  of euphoric elation;
 "ending" times,
  where "goodbye" is said far too early.

Jesus implied such things
   when two disciples asked
     "Teacher, where are you staying?"
He answered enigmatically, symbolically:
     "Come, and you will see."
Thus began the journey of a lifetime
   for these two questioning seekers.

Jesus knew that life, like faith,
   does not come prepackaged
   with easy answers and quick solutions;
   nor are life's destinations
     always obvious,
   or supposed "goals"
     what they are perceived to be.
The journeys of faith-filled lives
   are never so much about
     getting there
   but more about
     how people get there—
and what wisdom they learn
   along the way.

Abraham journeyed to a "promised land"—
   and became father to a nation
     along the way.
Moses' fantastic journey led to freedom—
   freed from slavery
   and free to serve the Liberator.
Matthew's magi followed a tedious journey—
   years of scanning stars
   that led to a simple stable in Bethlehem.
Jesus' journey led to a cross outside Jerusalem—
   and to giving his life
     as redemption for sin.
Along the way,
   we were invited to join—
"Come and follow me."

Take a long look at your faith today.
Whether it be long and tedious
    like the magi,
or short and simple
    like the shepherds,
still the faith journey must be made—
a journey of moving toward God,
    away from sin and fear,
a journey of walking in trust and Love,
    despite pain and disappointment.

Life's greatest lessons are learned
    more in the battle-scarred wisdom
        gained "on the road"
    than in the ease of comfortable routine;
    more in taking risk-filled steps
        toward God
    than in standing still, stagnating in fear;
    more in journeying in trust
        with Jesus to Glory
    than in waiting for God
        to hit you over the head.

Choose to see faith
    as a journey back "home"
        where you belong.
Take God as your constant companion
    wherever life may call you.
Take courage daily
    in the power God gives.
Always keep God
    as the center of every life event.

Choose to grow in your faith
    as you walk through this world.
What is the last spiritual book you read?
The last time you read Scripture?
Volunteered for an important cause?

Unless your inner spirit grows,
   learns "on the road"—
life's journey
   will have been for naught.

Always remember life's ultimate Goal—
   focus on the Glory to come
      not on the tumult at hand.
Keep your eyes on the Prize—
   for it is indeed
   "the pearl of great price."

Baptized in Love

Baptism of the Lord

(Luke 3:15–22)

People often use the phrase
　　"baptism in fire"
　　to signify beginnings that are
　　rough, challenging, and difficult.
A person newly hired
　　is often thrown into a job
　　without much training or experience.
Soldiers newly arrived to the front
　　often are marched straight into battle,
　　literally being "baptized in fire."
How people are "baptized"—
　　how they initiate and begin
　　the major events of their life—
　　has immense impact on
　　　　their entire life.

The very beginning of life itself
　　offers a perfect example.
Does one get baptized into nurturing love—
　　into gentleness yet firmness,
　　compassion yet structure,
　　faith yet freedom?

Or is there baptism into dysfunction—
    into discipline without controls,
    rigidity without compassion,
    surrounded by addiction and absence?
"Train a child in the way he should go;
    when he is old he will not turn from it" (Proverbs 22:6).

It is highly significant
    that Jesus began his "career"
    the way many of us began life—
    with a religious baptism.
It was a baptism in water,
    customary for that time and place,
    but highly symbolic in deeper meaning.
Jesus was truly "baptized in love"—
    affirmed in his uniqueness
    by a beloved Father,
    confirmed in a special call
    by the Spirit of power.
"A voice from heaven was heard:
    'You are my beloved Son.
    On you my favor rests'" (Luke 3:22).

Because of this baptism in love,
    Jesus was able to minister
    in complete and utter confidence—
    with boldness, courage, and mercy,
    freed from fear, ego, and lust,
    to be totally about
        "his Father's business."
Empowered by that archetypal baptism,
    Jesus Christ could
        confront religious hypocrites,
        upset people's plans and prejudices,
        challenge the social order—
    and ultimately die for his beliefs.

You may find this hard to believe—
　　but your baptism has the Power
　　to do the same for you.

When you were baptized,
　　the same words of the Father
　　were spoken to you:
"You are my beloved.
　　On you my favor rests" (Luke 3:22).
You, too, were "baptized in love,"
　　confirmed in goodness, value, and worth,
　　in your total uniqueness in this universe.
You, too, are God's "beloved"—
　　"with whom he is well pleased."

When you were baptized,
　　the same power of the Spirit
　　flowed in and through you.
"He will baptize you
　　in the Holy Spirit and fire."
You, too, have a divine Energy within,
　　a fire of potential and promise,
　　a capacity for greatness
　　　in your actions and words.
"Greater is the One within you,
　　than the one that is in the world" (1 John 4:4).

This is the truth
　　of how you were "baptized" into life,
　　of how your existence began.
In the beginning, there was no fear—
　　no uncertainty or confusion,
　　no doubt or inadequacy.
These are purely human things
　　you have picked up in this world.

No matter what your human beginnings were,
   your spiritual baptism
   was one of Love and Power.
You were surrounded by Love,
   empowered by Mercy,
   entrusted with Power,
   authorized by God.
Knowing this now, go forth
   to walk in confidence,
   to speak in humbleness,
   to live in love,
   to act in justice
      each and every day!

The Illogic of God

Second Sunday in Ordinary Time

(Isaiah 62:1–5; Zechariah 4:6; John 2:1–12)

Modern society, business, and culture
    are focused on "the practical."
        Will it work?
        Is this practical?
        Will it make money?
        Will it sell?

Yet God's ways of working in people's lives,
    God's *modus operandi*,
        what is usual for him—
    is extremely *unusual*
        to most of the world!
God's ways utterly defy
    common sense and logic.
    They confound our sense
        of practicality.

In Isaiah 62, Israel had consistently disobeyed.
The nation had forgotten God,
    had "forsaken their land"—
yet what does our illogical God say to them?
    "You are my beloved, my delight!"

In John 2, at a wedding reception in Cana,
    when his own mother asked for help,
    Jesus made a paradoxical request—
        "Fill these jars with water."
Knowing the ways of her Son and his Father,
    her wise instructions that day two thousand years ago
    are a gem of wisdom through the ages—
        "Do whatever he tells you."
The resulting wine was a shock to everyone.

The Bible and history
    are full of such stories:
    the father of the Jewish nation
        called to brutally sacrifice his only son,
    an aged, barren, old woman
        giving birth to a prophet called the "Baptist,"
    a stubborn headstrong fisherman
        becoming Jesus' chosen leader.

All this reveals one simple fact:
    God's ways are not our ways!
"As far as the heavens
    are above the earth,
    are my ways above your ways,
    and my thoughts
        above your thoughts" (Isaiah 55:9).
God's ways of working
    rarely seem to make sense.
They go against the prideful logic
    of human wisdom
    and challenge our overvalued
        common sense.

Yet we routinely presume
    that because our limited logic
    makes perfect sense and seems
        to explain things,

God must have the same logic,
the same pattern of thinking,
the same mode of acting
   as we humans do.
What arrogance!
What audacity to presume
   that God must think and act
     the same way his creation does!

God's ways are ways of faith not logic.
   "We walk by faith not by sight."
Divine actions always lie
   beyond human comprehension—
   for example, the action of a Son
     dying on a cross
   bringing Life to many
     who couldn't care less.

God's ways always reflect
   Reasons beyond eternity,
   Wisdom beyond knowledge,
     Power beyond logic.

Open your mind
   to the unfathomable Mystery
   that we call Yahweh,
   Allah,
   Father,
     God.
Allow yourself to float freely
   without preconception or preoccupation,
   without plan or presumption
   in the sea of illogical,
     infinite Mercy
   that is the Wisdom of your God.

Give up your problems and concerns
    to the Infinite One—
    and know that what you *want*
        is one thing,
    what God knows you *need*
        is another.
"God's grace is sufficient
    for all your needs" (2 Corinthians 12:9).

Open your inner spirit
    to receive unexpected blessings—
    gifts and insights that come
        in different forms than expected,
        in different time frames than planned.
All life's greatest gifts
    come at unprepared times,
        in truly unusual ways.

"Keep your eyes open—
    the Son of man will come
    at a time you least expect" (Luke 12:40).

Power of the Word

Third Sunday in Ordinary Time

(Nehemiah 8:2–10; Luke 1:1–4; 4:14–21)

The written word is civilization's
  greatest tool, gift, and power.
Books have a power to change lives—
  a tool spurring growth and progress.
The gift of words written and printed
  has transformed all our world.
"Ezra read out of the book
  from daybreak to midday;
  all the people listened attentively
  to the book of the law" (Nehemiah 8:3–4).

When God wanted to tell us about himself,
  he could have chosen many different ways.
But God chose to speak words—
  to talk to humans about his ways,
  about his plans and dreams,
  his love and passion for us.
"God spoke to our forefathers
  at many times and in various ways . . .
  but in these last days,
  he has spoken to us
    through his Son" (Hebrews 1:1–2).

God spoke words to us
    about every aspect of life—
    how to find peace within ourselves,
    how to live in this world,
    where our destiny lies,
      and who God is.

Inspired writers later captured
    many of those powerful messages,
    and compiled them into a sacred text—
    the holy Scriptures,
    the living Word of the Lord.
"Many have undertaken to compile
    a narrative of the events
    which have been fulfilled in our midst.
I too have carefully traced
    the sequence from the beginning . . . " (Luke 1:1–3).

Ever since that time,
    God's words have a special place
    in the lives of true believers.
God's own words are words
    of comfort and challenge,
    peace and power.
God's words can soothe a troubled soul,
    calm an angry heart,
    bring peace in the midst of grief.

God's words are different from human words—
    they have a power to *effect*
    what they convey.

"God's word is living and effective,
sharper than any two-edged sword.
It penetrates and divides soul and spirit . . .
it judges the reflections and thoughts
of the heart" (Hebrews 4:12).

To follow Jesus more nearly,
    and respond more clearly
    to his challenging message,
    you must know God's words.
They must become real to you,
    living realities in your life,
    touching every part of your self.
"The people were weeping
    as they heard the words of the law.
Ezra said 'Do not be saddened,
    for rejoicing in the Lord
    must be your strength!'" (Nehemiah 8:10)

Jesus found his own mission
    uniquely expressed and witnessed
    in the prophetic words of Isaiah.
The Son of God spent hours
    reflecting on these words—
    words written by humans
    but inspired by his Father.
"Today this Scripture passage
    is fulfilled in your hearing."

God's Word is guide for your actions,
    inspiration for your vision,
    challenge to your stubbornness,
    hope in your sadness,
        and Life for your spirit.

Read the Word.
Study it diligently.
Sit quietly with it.
Pray with it.
Allow God's Word to touch
    your deepest soul and spirit.

God's Spokespersons

Fourth Sunday in Ordinary Time

(Jeremiah 1:4–5,17–19; 1 Corinthians 12:31–13:13; Luke 4:21–30)

When I was a boy (many years ago),
    I loved being able to say to my brother
    "Mom says to do it!"
When my mom delegated me
    to pass on some particular message,
    I felt specially empowered and unique.

Two thousand years ago,
    when Jesus walked this earth,
    he called people to follow him,
      spoke words of wisdom to them,
      challenged them,
      empowered them,
      healed them.
In essence, he was a prophet,
    a spokesperson for the Almighty,
    speaking messages sometimes challenging,
      sometimes consoling,
    but always in touch with the One who sent him.
"The word you hear is not mine;
    it comes from the Father who sent me."

When Jesus left this world,
    he delegated others to carry on this work—
    disciples who would speak the words of God
        in future generations,
        to children yet unborn,
        to generations yet unforeseen.

To this very day,
    Jesus continues to choose others
    for this vital task—
        namely us!!
"Before I formed you in the womb I knew you;
    before you were born I dedicated you,
    a prophet to the nations
        I appointed you" (Jeremiah 1:5).

We are God's spokespersons,
    his twenty-first century apostles,
    the ones delegated to continue his mission
of bringing God's words
        to this wounded earth.
This is a humbling, daunting task,
    undertaken only by humble hearts,
    wrapped in daily prayer,
    empowered by others in Love.

The divine message the world needs today
    is one that demands of the spokesperson
        quiet listening,
        soulful reflection.
Indeed one's personal intelligence,
    and one's human words
    (motivated by pride and ego)
    may get in the way of God's words.

"If I speak with human tongues and angelic as well,
   but do not have love,
   I am a noisy gong,
     a clanging cymbal" (1 Corinthians 13:1).

The message we bring is simply this—
   "God's power can change lives!
The mercy and compassion of God
   can change *your* life!
God's love is patient yet powerful,
   challenging yet consoling.
Find God—and find true peace."
"Greater is he that is in you,
   than he that is in the world" (John 4:4).

These are the words God needs you to share.
You are a spokesperson of this divine message,
   this surpassingly simple mystery of Love.
You are a spokesperson of Good News
   in a world filled with bad news.
"Gird your loins—stand up
   and tell them all I command you!" (Jeremiah 1:17)

Jesus Christ has no hands today but yours,
   no feet today but yours,
   no voice today but yours.
Spread God's word,
   live God's word,
   speak the word
   to all the world that will listen.
Tell them that we have a great God
   who is with us always,
     in all ways!

"Go therefore, make disciples of all the nations.
Teach them everything I have commanded you.
And know that I am with you always,
* until the end of the world!"* (Matthew 28:19–20)

Involved or Committed?

Fifth Sunday in Ordinary Time

(Isaiah 6:1–8; 1 Corinthians 15:1–11; Luke 5:1–11)

A farmer friend told me one day,
"Faith is like breakfast—
   like the difference
   between bacon and eggs.
A chicken laying an egg—
   that's involvement;
   but a pig giving bacon—
   that's commitment!"

Our world and its churches
   are filled with involved people,
   people active in many ways:
      school, society, family, business.
Some are involved in worthwhile causes,
   some attend church regularly,
   some share time and talent freely.
People are busier and more involved today,
   more active and occupied,
   than at any time in history.

But while hell is full of "involved people,"
    heaven will be populated by "committed people."
The problem with "involvement" is
    it can become shallow and superficial—
    full of empty actions and powerless words.
The power of "commitment"
    is that it involves our deepest soul and spirit—
    signifying lasting values not passing fancies.
"Jesus said to the Twelve 'Will you also leave me?'
    Simon Peter answered, 'Lord to whom shall we go?
    You have the words of eternal life'" (John 6:67–68).

People who make commitments go beyond externals;
    they act out of love or faith or trust—
    because life's greatest values
    can never be seen, heard, tasted, or touched,
    but only grasped in courage and boldness.
"I heard the voice of the Lord saying,
    'Whom shall I send? Who will go for us?'
    'Here I am,' I said, 'send me!'" (Isaiah 6:8).

People who make commitments
    are not without fears and doubts,
    yet consciously choose to act anyway—
    trusting in the wisdom of friends,
        the surety of conscience,
        and the power of faith.
People who make commitments
    courageously say "Yes!"
    while others are saying "I don't know."

It takes courage to make a commitment—
    perhaps that is why many fear to do so today.
But take a lesson from history:
    the greatest leaders were those
    who chose clearly and faithfully
    when others wavered and feared.

Men like Isaiah the prophet—
   whose mouth was burned
   by a white-hot coal
   making him worthy to preach.

Men like Paul the preacher—
   shipwrecked, stoned, beaten, imprisoned—
   all for the sake
   of the Good News he preached.

Women like Mary Magdalene—
   a reformed prostitute
   who turned her whole life around
   when she met her Master.

Are you involved or committed?
Is there anything in life you hold to
   so passionately,
   so deeply,
   that you would lay down your life for it?
God has already revealed his commitment—
   it is to us, forever, for life.
Out of total love for you,
   his only Son died on a cross.

Have you made your commitment to God,
   the Creator who loved you to life—
   or are you just occasionally "involved"
   when it's convenient for you?
Are you willing to imitate Simon Peter,
   who (despite a long night's work)
   returned to the lake in total faith
   upon the mere word of Jesus—
      and was rewarded by a huge catch.
*"Master we have been hard at it all night,
      but if you say so I will lower the nets"* (Luke 5:5).

Make some life commitments—
  commitments reflecting who you are
    and what you believe.
Make a personal commitment to God—
  the single most important commitment
    you will ever make.
The commitments you make
  will reveal your soul.

WEEK 13

The Be-Attitudes

Sixth Sunday in Ordinary Time

(Jeremiah 17:5–8; Luke 6:17, 20–26)

Following God seriously
   does not mean occasional prayers
   "tossed" heavenward,
   or a few charitable actions
     from time to time.
Following God
   is life-transforming work.
It means a true change in attitude,
   an inner transformation
     from ego-driven human actions
     to God-motivated spiritual reactions.

But changing our inner attitude,
   transforming a human heart,
   can be a most difficult challenge.
Wars, revolutions, and physical force
   may enslave and coerce the body,
     but cannot touch the heart.
Television shows, books, motivational tapes,
   may empower some in this world
   but often never touch
     the depths of inner denial.

49

Thankfully, God has a way
   to teach the human heart.
"You do not have a high priest
   who is unable to sympathize
      with our weaknesses" (Hebrews 4:15).

The earthly life of Jesus
   and his profound teachings
   are paradigms for transforming
      the human heart.
This God-Man has already modeled
   the exact approach needed
   to change human selfishness,
      and transform greed and pride.
Jesus teaches us "BE-attitudes"—
   attitudes born in the depths
      of his own divine personality;
   attitudes that teach us how to live and "be"
      more than to produce,
      consume, or achieve;
   attitudes that can transform and soften
      the dark stubbornness
      of the human heart.
"Your attitude should be
   the same as that
      of Jesus Christ" (Philippians 2:5).

You will be blessed
   when you are "poor in spirit":
   humbled in your inner spirit
      by the awesome presence of your Creator;
   gentle and patient with others,
   softened in ego and pride
      yet strong in spirit and purpose.
"God has chosen those who are poor . . .
   to be rich in faith
      and inherit the Kingdom" (James 2:5).

You will be blessed
　　when you are "hungry":
　　an unfamiliar feeling in modern America,
　　　　yet a desperate spiritual need;
　　an inner yearning
　　　　for the "full-filling" that only God can give;
　　a spiritual craving
　　　　for the satisfying salvation of God
　　　　more than
　　　　the plaudits and praises of man.
"Seek first the Kingdom of God,
　　and all else will be given you besides" (Matthew 6:33).

You will be blessed when you "weep":
　　mourning a lack of personal faithfulness
　　　　more than shallow losses
　　　　or personal comfort;
　　crying over the modern dearth of eternal values
　　　　more than the personal losses
　　　　that are part of human life;
　　grieving society's injustice and prejudice,
　　　　and actively working
　　　　to "stand in the gap,"
　　　　to make a difference.
"I come to cast a fire on the earth,
　　and I wish it were burning brightly!" (Luke 12:49)

But "woe to you" who obsess
　　about the peripheral things—
　　　　wealth, success, power, fame,
　　　　money, clothing, cars, or cash.
Enjoy the temporary comforts
　　you possess in this moment
　　for eternal comfort and peace
　　may elude you.
"Woe to you" who seek to be full
　　of the "best" of this world,
　　who laugh at serious commitment

to God, to work, or to another,
who obsess about fame, good name,
   "playing the game"—
for you will reap the folly
   of the shallowness
   you have sown.

"Your attitude should be the same
   as that of Jesus Christ" (Philippians 2:5).
Allow Jesus to begin to transform
   your attitudes into
   his "be-attitudes."
Give God permission to move freely
   in the hidden depths
      of your inner world,
   "that he may increase
      and you may decrease" (John 3:30).

"The Hardest Thing"

Seventh Sunday in Ordinary Time

(1 Samuel 26:2–23; Psalm 103; Luke 6:27–38)

What is the hardest thing
   God has ever asked you to do?

Let go of a beloved in death?
Watch someone struggle with a burden
   and you're unable to help?
Care for an aging parent
   when, for so many years,
     she took care of you?
Or could it perhaps be
   taking Jesus at his word
     when he says
   "Love your enemies,
   do good to those who hate you,
   bless those who curse you,
   pray for those who mistreat you" (Luke 6:27f).

Forgiveness may be
   the most difficult thing
   we are ever called to do
     in this entire world.

Taking Jesus' word seriously,
 "forgiving others as God forgives us,"
 when part of us wants to say,
  "This doesn't apply to me,"
  "I have a *right* not to forgive"—
 this is a risk.
The challenge of forgiveness
 may be our greatest challenge
 in following the wisdom
 we call "Good News"
 and living a truly God-centered lifestyle.

But yet, forgiveness is the key
 to traversing the "deep waters"
  of falling into God.
It is always an enormous risk
 to forgive one who has hurt us,
 to love those who do not care for us,
 to let go of a resentment,
 to move past long-harbored bitterness,
 to allow an angry grudge to be forgotten,
 even forgive ourselves—
 for mistakes and inadequacies,
 for needless guilt.
These are the challenges to deeper growth.

But it is safe to say
 that all true spiritual development,
 every new level of healing,
 will somehow embrace
  these dark truths.

There are three reasons why the
 divine wisdom of forgiveness
 is absolutely necessary for life.
First, bitter unforgiveness and anger
 can kill us.

Long-held hatred and bitterness
    is a cancer growing within—
    it consumes and destroys,
    twisting the human spirit
        beyond recognition.
    "'Vengeance is mine,' says the Lord"
    (Deuteronomy 32:35).

Second, the greatest motive for forgiveness
    and for letting go of grudges, anger, and bitterness
    comes from beyond this world.
It is simply this:
    our God has already forgiven us.
Wisdom simply asks that *we* do
    as our Creator God
        has already done for us.
"Be compassionate,
    as your Father is compassionate" (Luke 6:36).
"This is my commandment:
    love one another
    as I have loved you" (John 15:12).

Last, the words of Jesus himself
    hauntingly foreshadow our eternity.
"Pardon, and you will be pardoned.
Give and it will be given back to you.
For the measure you measure with
    will be measured back to you" (Luke 6:37–38).

Face life's most difficult challenge—
    learn the divine wisdom of letting go,
        and choose to forgive.
Forgiveness is indeed a choice,
    not a feeling.
It is a simple act of the will—
    a decision of the heart—
    to release and reconcile
    with those who have hurt you.

———

Choose to surround these people
   with a bubble of light and love:
  a light that dispels
    the darkness of resentment,
  and a love that sets you
    and them
    free.

Forgiveness will free your soul,
   release the Spirit,
  steer you
    to eternal peace.

The Fruit of Your Tree

Eighth Sunday in Ordinary Time

(Sirach 27:4–7; Luke 6:39–45)

Growing up in western Michigan,
    I was surrounded by fruit orchards:
    apple, cherry, and peach trees
    grew within yards of our house.
As a child, I learned to tell what a tree was like
    by examining the fruit it produced.

Only later in life did I realize
    that this experience taught me
    a valuable spiritual lesson.
One Old Testament wise man said,
    *"The fruit of a tree shows
    the care it has had"* (Sirach 27:6).
Jesus used the identical image, saying,
    "Each tree is known by its fruit" (Luke 6:44).

Each of us is like a tree
    in the vast orchard created by our God.

We have been placed here on earth,
   lovingly planted as a small seed,
   sowed with purpose in good ground,
    by the divine Farmer.
We were then gently cared for—
   watered, nourished, and fertilized,
   painfully pruned at times,
   cut back and trimmed to size—
   all for the single purpose
    of bearing good fruit.

"A good man brings good things
   out of the good stored up in his heart;
   an evil man brings evil things
   out of the evil stored in his heart.
For out of the overflow of his heart,
   a person's mouth speaks" (Luke 6:45).

What is the fruit of your tree like?
God has put much time, love, and effort
   into your growth and maturity—
   now God, the divine Farmer,
   looks to your tree expectantly,
   searching for the good fruit
    that will nourish others.
Your words, your actions, your commitments—
   these are the fruits of the tree
   of spiritual walking with the Lord.
"A person's speech discloses
   the bent of his mind" (Sirach 27:6).

Does your manner of speaking reflect
   the way the Lord would speak?
Is there undue sarcasm, cynicism,
   pessimism, racism, gossip, or meddling
   in your dialogue with others?

Do your everyday actions and gestures
    reflect the way Jesus would act?
Is there undue rudeness, insensitivity, injustice,
    rashness, bitterness, or self-centeredness
    in your dealings with others?

Is the fruit of your tree
    mature, ripe, and juicy—
    fruit that blesses and encourages,
    uplifts and nourishes?

Or is the product of your tree
    flat, bitter, or spoiled—
    bruised by greed, lust, or envy,
    rotted with ego and pride?
"Every tree that does not bear good fruit
    is cut down and thrown into the fire" (Matthew 7:19).

Take good care of the tree
    of your spirituality and faith.
Nourish it daily with prayer,
    fertilize it with God's Word,
    feed it with works of justice and peace,
    enrich it with silent simplicity,
    water it with humble faithfulness.

Spend time pruning your spiritual tree.
Cut away shoots of stinginess or selfishness,
    pull up weeds of greed and dishonesty,
    trim back excessive control and ego.

Learn to become a good fruit inspector!
Check the fruit of your words and actions
    each night before you sleep.
"By their fruits you shall recognize them" (Matthew 7:20).

*"The fruit of the Spirit is
    love, joy, peace, patient endurance,
    kindness, generosity, faith,
    mildness and chastity"* (Galatians 5:22).

Deal with Your Demons!

First Week of Lent

(Genesis 2:7–9, 3:1–7; Luke 4:1–2)

Have you ever been to a desert?
There is a unique "hard beauty" there—
the dry, barren beauty of life
toughened by sand and solitude.

After a "baptism in love,"
Jesus walked into the desert
to face his demons—
for the desert wilderness
symbolizes the need
to wrestle with the dark sides of one's life.

There is a lesson here for us:
if the Lord of the Universe,
the King of Kings himself,
felt it essential to wrestle
with the dark forces of this world—
why should it be different for us?

Do not run from those dark sides,
  those shadow places of yourself—
  compulsions, fears, prejudices,
  dark angers, and urges that may lurk within.
With God as your Anchor, face your fears.
Walk forward into the darkness
  of the inner desert,
  but take Jesus
    as companion and Light.

The demons of the desert
  that Jesus had to deal with
  may be the same you wrestle with.
"He was tempted in every way we are,
  yet was without sin" (Hebrews 4:15).

Jesus was tempted to turn stones to bread:
  a temptation to excessive security,
  to fully gratify
    all human senses and needs,
  to grow comfortable,
    at ease in this world.
"But not by bread alone
  is man to live . . . " (Deuteronomy 8:3).
  For God's words alone
    give true peace.
The world can offer
  only conditional comforts.
Seek the true Peace
  that passes understanding.

Jesus was tempted
  to throw himself off the Temple:
  a temptation to abuse power and control,
  to dominate and misuse,
  to exploit and intimidate,
  to excessively control people, things, life.

"Do not put the Lord to the test."
"You shall worship God alone" (Deuteronomy 6:16).
The first Power in life, work, family,
   is always God.
Seek the true Power
      that lies in a humble heart.

Jesus was tempted to homage the Evil One:
   a temptation to privilege and entitlement,
   to a painless, suffering-free salvation,
   to be somehow exempt
      from life's struggles and conflicts.
"You shall do homage
to the Lord your God" (Deuteronomy 6:13).
   Jesus honored his Father's plan,
      "emptying himself even to death" (Philippians 2:7–8).

The "poor in spirit" know what the rich cannot:
   suffering for God leads
      to salvation with God.
Seek the Poverty
   of utter reliance upon God.

How Jesus faced his demons is a lesson:
   walk forward into your fears,
   stay grounded in God,
   remain rooted in the Truth
      of the Father's love for you.
The Light of Truth will indeed "set you free"—
   but you must be content
   being uncomfortable for a time!

Have no fear when darkness descends
    and you wrestle with your dark sides.
Know this truth—
    you never go alone into darkness,
    for "I am with you always!"
You are anchored
    to a Rock of strength!

Making Heaven Your Home

Second Week of Lent

(Genesis15:5–18; Philippians 3:17–4:1; Luke 9:28–36)

Imagine for a moment
   all your dreams fulfilled,
   all your hopes realized,
   all your ambitions attained!

Then imagine this as well:
   all fears and doubts,
   apprehensions and uncertainties,
   dissolved in one blinding flash
      of surpassing serenity.
What complete ecstasy this would be!

This happened one day two thousand years ago.
Three men were with their Teacher—
   the One they'd come to trust and love—
   men named Peter, James, and John.
As their Master prayed that day,
   high on a mountain nearby,
   an astonishing transformation occurred.

"While he was praying,
    his face changed in appearance
    and his clothes became dazzingly white.
Suddenly two men appeared with Him . . .
    they appeared in glory . . . " (Luke 9:29–30)
For the briefest of moments,
    God brought a little bit of heaven
    to the humble earth of Galilee.
God lifted a corner of the veil
    separating heaven's infinite glories
    from earth's finite frustrations—
    and three astonished apostles
    were never again the same.

The goal of our human journey
    is, in the end, absurdly simple—
    life with God in heaven forever,
    sharing that same divine vision forever.
This is the entire purpose for life,
    the very reason for our existence,
    the divine destiny
        planted deep in our soul.
"We have our citizenship
    in heaven . . . " (Philippians 3:20)

Heaven is eternal peace and healing restoration,
    eternal ecstasy and union in Love.
It is the conviction millions have died for—
    and should be the goal we live for.
But there is only one entry point
    into heaven's glory and peace:
    the doorway of death.

Death in our physical body certainly,
    but more importantly,
    a slower more painful death—
    a death to self
        each day of our life.

"No one can see the reign of God
unless he is born again from above" (John 3:3).

This death and rebirth requires
    a letting go of one's self,
    yielding up of one's ego,
    reaching out beyond self
        in justice and compassion,
    moving past attainment or achievement
        to reach divine awareness,
    falling in love
        with the God of Peter, James, and John.

Gospel singer Mahalia Jackson sings
    about working to make heaven her home.

Dying to self in this world
    to reach heaven's ecstasy in the next
    is "work" as difficult as any
    we will ever do in this world.

We can work to "make heaven our home"
    by living and acting in love
        twenty-four hours a day,
    by enduring patiently
        the burdens uniquely ours,
    by taking actions
        for justice and equality,
    by putting God
        in the first place of our life.

Always remember your divine destiny,
    the glorious goal awaiting you
    at the end of all life's challenges!
Always keep your eyes on the prize—
    and work daily "to make heaven your home"!

"How lovely is your dwelling place,
  O Lord God of hosts.
One day within your courts
  is better than a thousand elsewhere!" (Psalm 84:10)

Fat and Sassy

Third Week of Lent

(1 Corinthians 10:1–6, 10–12)

We are truly a "fast food generation."
    We grab quick convenient meals,
    mass-produced hamburgers,
    deep-fried french fries,
    a diet drink
        (we *are* watching our calories)
    as we race along our busy paths.
Children grow up today skipping breakfast,
    eating boxed school lunches,
    grabbing anything available for dinner.
Doctors have for years spoken
    of the long-range negative effects
    of such unhealthy eating habits,
    and likely most of us know this.

But in our spiritual lives,
    many fall into the same unhealthy lifestyle—
    fast routine prayers (if any)
    with little depth
        and minimal spiritual growth.

We have become a "fast-faith generation" as well—
    shortened prayers
        match our quickened lives,
    rushed Scripture study
        but increased TV viewing,
    ignored works of charity
        yet always time for what we want to do.

Just as doctors warn us
    about the physical effects
    of unhealthy eating
        in a "fast-food" age,
    so becoming a "fast-faith" generation
    can be just as deadly
        to our spiritual health.

Why is it that people today
    are so concerned with physical diets,
    with personal health and eating habits,
    yet ignore their spiritual health—
    their unhealthy "fast-faith" lifestyles,
    and the eternal stakes
        involved with "soul-health"?

The apostle Paul says today,
    "They all ate spiritual food
    and drank spiritual drink
    but God was not pleased" (1 Corinthians 10:4–5).
Just as fast food eventually hardens arteries,
    so too shallow, routine faith
    and long-ignored spirituality
        hardens the soul
        and clogs spiritual arteries.

It is easy for the most spiritual of us
    to become fat in blindness,
    sassy in overconfidence,
    convinced of our righteous lifestyle.
Remember the words of Jesus though:
"This people honors me
    with their lips,
    but their hearts
    are far from me" (Mark 7:6).

Do not get "fat and sassy"
    in your spiritual health.

Work at remaining constantly open
    to the Spirit's gentle movements,
    flexible to the Spirit's quiet promptings.

Remain healthy by daily prayer time.
Spend quality time daily
    with the One who has Power
    to transform the rest of your day.

Build up your "Spirit wisdom"
    by regular Scripture study,
    quiet meditation,
    reflective reading.

Deepen your faith
    by going out of yourself
    in regular weekly worship,
    communing with the larger
        Body of Christ.

"Let a person examine himself first
and then eat the bread
and drink the cup.
For he that eats and drinks unworthily
drinks damnation
to themselves" (1 Corinthians 10:28–29).

Coming Back Home

Fourth Week of Lent

(Luke 15:1–3, 11–32)

In years of traveling the Midwest,
    there is always a special joy for me
    at crossing the Michigan state line,
    returning to my birthplace to see family.
At one time or another,
    most people have experienced this—
    the joy of "coming back home."

But however we "come back home"—
    whether to a birthplace,
    to an area evoking sweet memories,
    to a beloved person,
    or to God's love and forgiveness—
    humbleness, grace, and wisdom are required.
"Grace-full returning" demands that we
    admit our loss, brokenness, and pain,
    and acknowledge any sinful isolation
        caused by "separation."

In this famous "prodigal son" story,
    the younger son
    consciously chose to separate himself
    from his family of birth.
Perhaps you can relate to that choice
    to depart from your roots,
    to cut yourself off
    from that which nourished you for years.
Separateness can mean many things.
    For some, a wise and mature life choice,
    for others, a selfish foolhardy decision,
    for many, a confusing mixture of both.
"Choose this day who you will serve . . . " (Joshua 24:15)

There is always one danger lurking in separation:
    the risk of alienation—
    a premature severing
        of important life-connections,
    a precipitate turning away
        from unappreciated life wisdom.
Too often human separations are
    more dangerous overreactions
    than conscious, independent choices.
Simply put, we often leave
    before we've learned the lesson.

Beware of "people alienations"—
    separations that happen quickly,
        and often far too easily,
    between family and friends.
Do not let them become irreparable,
    frozen in hurt, charged with negativity.
Never get trapped by negative emotions
    of resentment, bitterness, anger.

But the worst alienations
    are between us and God—
    because there is absolutely
    no reason for them.
We can always "come back home" to God
    when we've fallen short or failed,
    despite personal errors, mistakes, or sin.

Luke's Gospel portrays God as a nervous father,
    watching and waiting for his son's return,
    rejoicing when he sees him.
"When still a long way off,
    his father caught sight of him
    and was deeply moved" (Luke 15:20).

But first the separated son had to
    admit the wounds of his separation,
    acknowledge his sin of alienation,
    and humbly ask forgiveness.
"Father I have sinned
    against God and you . . . " (Luke 15:21)
These actions in themselves had power—
    restoring the broken bonds
    of blessing and brotherhood
    between father and son.

Where do you need to confront
    separation in your life?
Where have you "broken away" and left
    before you learned the lesson?

Where do you perhaps need to break away,
    yet continue to hold on in fear or insecurity?
Where and with whom do you experience
    the cold resentment of alienation?

Work at "coming home" grace-fully—
    with humble recognition of your failures,
    with honest acceptance of hard realities,
    with gentleness and grace,
        not rancor or resentment.
Recognize the need
    to "come back home" in your heart
    before coming back to any person or place.
Know that you always have Power
    to undo separations in God's world.
Remember that your God is always waiting.

The Gift of Guilt

Fifth Week of Lent

(Psalm 51; Romans 8:23; John 8:1–11)

Guilt. Shame for one's failings.
There are no more thoroughly dismissed,
    completely discounted concepts,
    in modern American culture.
In our current "sophisticated" society,
    guilt is a "useless appendage
    of an outdated culture."
It is never anyone's fault today.
Few people admit guilt or blame.

The modern trend is "spinning the truth"—
    deflecting personal blame
    or admission of wrongdoing
    to someone or something else.
"Society and genetics made me do it."
    "My enemies are trying to ruin me."
    "You shouldn't have served the coffee so hot."
Tools to deny guilt today include
    self-justifying lawsuits,
    self-obsessed psychology,
    self-centered mock indignation,
    a total vacuum of personal integrity.

Jesus Christ gives us many things,
  but the most unappreciated gift
  is the gift of healthy guilt.
The story of a woman caught in adultery
  teaches our world timeless truths.
We are created as good and beautiful beings,
  yet weak and prideful by nature.
One can never truly be at peace
  while unacknowledged sin lurks within.
"For I know my weakness,
  my sin is before me always" (Psalm 51:5).

Our inner spirit can never be one with God
  while unacknowledged defects of character,
  unowned personal flaws and failures,
  remain purposefully hidden,
  denied and buried deep within.
Wrongdoing will burden one's soul,
  until relieved by confession.
Unacknowledged offenses block divine movement
  until admitted before God, self, and others.

Healthy guilt is a humble, honest attitude
  that is completely unself-centered.
It acknowledges personal brokenness,
  confesses weakness, lust, ego, and pride—
  seeking only the divine Freedom
    found in sincere forgiveness,
  searching only for the real Truth
    found in brutal self-honesty.
"Confess your sins,
  and believe the Good News!" (Mark 1:15)

Healthy guilt does not mean obsessive shame,
  compulsive self-blaming,
  or perennially degrading one's self.
Jesus simply said to the woman,
  "Neither do I condemn you."

When God forgives, God forgets.
When God does not obsess about sin,
   humans need not obsess about guilt.

Julian of Norwich said it well:
"The Lord looks on his servants
   with pity and not with blame.
In God's sight we do not fall,
   in our sight, we do not stand.
Both of these are true,
   but the deeper insight belongs to God"
    (*Revelations of Divine Love*, #82).

Healthy guilt is honesty and humility:
   taking ownership over your actions;
   taking charge of your defects and flaws;
   taking Jesus at his word—
    "Go and sin no more!"

Healthy guilt is recognizing
   the "gift of guilt"—
   that tug of conscience
   pulling you within yourself
   to humble, honest self-analysis.
"Behold, you are pleased
   with sincerity of heart" (Psalm 51:8).

Acknowledge the unacknowledged within—
   any shame, embarrassment, guilt,
    arising from your conscience,
   any inner gaps and burdens
    coming from sin and failure.
Bring these burdens and troubles
   to the One
    whose "grace is sufficient
    for all your needs."

Find the "peace that passes understanding"
   that comes from humbly admitting sin,
   honestly confronting self,
   hopefully embracing the freedom,
   the passionate forgiveness,
   the mercy and compassion
     of your great God.

"The Stones Will Shout"

Palm Sunday

(Luke's Passion, 22:14–23:56)

*"If they keep quiet,
the stones will shout out . . . "* (Luke 19:40)
Have you ever noticed the seeming
"conspiracy of silence"
about God in our modern world?

God's name cannot be mentioned
in America's public schools—
schools ironically founded
on fundamental Christian values.
Laws prohibit the display
of crosses and statues
on public property.
Easter and Christmas
have been "Hallmark-ized"
with cute, secular
(and highly marketable) items.

Jesus Christ has been reduced to jewelry—
gold necklaces and decorative pins
worn as nonreligious ornaments.

What has this generation done
    to the God of the ages?
"Father forgive them;
    they do not know what they are doing" (Luke 23:23).

Jesus Christ may no longer be on the cross.
He may no longer have a parched, dry throat
    calling out, "I thirst!"
But our world has muted, muffled throats,
    and it thirsts desperately
        for that "voice crying in the wilderness."

At times, the world loses its voice entirely—
    lauding the saintly life of Mother Teresa
        yet ignoring the poverty that condemns millions;
    shamelessly marketing cars to cosmetics
        yet blind to racism in housing
        and life in the unborn.
God needs us to pierce this
    contemporary "conspiracy of silence."

The impact of that one cross on Calvary
    inverts all the world stands for:
    comforting the disturbed,
    disturbing the comfortable,
    healing the most savage of souls,
    calming the deepest of fears.
The death of the God-man Jesus,
    the chosen Prophet sent for salvation,
    shatters the world's schemes and fears.

If someone does not proclaim this truth,
    indeed cry it from the rooftops,
    "the stones will shout out."

The Power of this God-Man Jesus,
    the awesome inevitability of his message,
    can never be quieted or curtailed;
    but amazingly Jesus today has no voice
        except your own.
The Son of God has no audible words
    but the ones you speak in love.
The Son of Man has no physical body
    except the one you give him to use.
The Good Shepherd has no prophetic wisdom
    except the divine discernment you bring.

The Creator is desperately in need
    of your words and actions
    to break the "conspiracy of silence"
    about the greatest Truth in existence.

God needs your voice to announce,
    "Ecce homo! Behold the Man!
    Truly this man was the Son of God."
God needs your tongue to proclaim,
    "Turn away from sin
    and believe the Good News."
God needs your lips to shout,
    "Love one another
    as I have loved you!"
God needs your words crying out,
    "Seek first the Kingdom of God,
    and all else will be given you as well."

The Creator needs modern prophets and apostles—
    ones who will speak his name
    and witness his values
    in the modern market places
        of mass media,
        of classrooms,
        of boardrooms.

Resolve during this Holy Week,
　　the week we honor Jesus' death,
　　to give witness to your faith.
Resolve to speak by your actions,
　　to lead by example
　　(and perhaps even words)
　　to the awesome mystery,
　　the awful majesty
　　of a God dying for his people
　　　out of love.

Stagnancy and Renewal

Easter

(Genesis 1:1–2:2; Exodus 14:15–15:1; Luke 24:1–12)

Stagnant water.
Few things in life
    are more unappealing
    than these pools absent of life.
Cluttered with decaying leaves
    and fallen branches,
    unmoving and unclean,
    untouched even by animals,
    stagnant water is near worthless.

But stagnancy is not limited
    to lifeless pools of water;
    far sadder is the way
    people can stagnate
    in similar ways,
    with similar results.
When human beings get mired
    in dead routines,
    in unhealthy excess
    or crippling worries,
    the same situation can occur.

Some seem to lead lives
　　of perpetual stagnation—
　　dreams long abandoned,
　　hopes replaced by disillusionment,
　　lives full of numbing boredom,
　　　mindless activity.
From time to time in life,
　　stagnancy happens to everyone—
　　a sense of lifelessness,
　　of deadness in one's spirit,
　　of intense frustration
　　　or deep loneliness.

But the human spirit,
　　divinely inspired and formed,
　　is tenacious and irrepressible!
God has created human beings
　　in a marvelously resilient way.
The waters of divine Life
　　flow constantly within us—
　　deep, strong, and clean,
　　refreshing and renewing
　　　the most stagnant situations.
Modeled after our own Maker,
　　we are made for Life not death.
"God created us in his image,
　　in the divine image he created us" (Genesis 1:27).

God's Life cannot be stopped!
There is always room for renewal,
　　rebirth, and revival in any situation
　　with a God to whom even death
　　　was not a barrier!
Transformation and change
　　is always possible
　　with our awesome God!

When confronted with impassable
"Red Seas" of problems and pain,
God calls us to *"go forward,"*
and *"know that I am the Lord"* (Exodus 14:14–18).

When the waters of this world
lead you into stagnation,
bringing you discouragement
or lifelessness—
return to the living waters
of the divine perspective,
the refreshing, renewing vision
that only God can give.
Do not search for life amidst places
where true life cannot be found.
"While still at a loss what to think,
two men appeared [and said]:
'Why do you search
for the living One
among the dead?
He is not here . . . '" (Luke 24:4–6)

Go to God first for Life—
then turn to take on
the problems of existence.
Renewed by the divine vision,
you will be better empowered
to confront what lies ahead.
Learn to see with God's eyes,
not with human emotions.

Draw upon hidden springs of Life—
your own inner goodness,
the words and wisdom of others,
the presence of loved ones.

Rid yourself of any
  "stinkin' thinkin'"—
thought patterns, people, or situations
that are negative, depressive, obsessive.
Put on a new attitude:
  imagine fresh waters of Life
  flowing through, in, around,
  every part of your being.
"Lay aside your old way of life,
  and acquire a fresh spiritual
    way of thinking" (Ephesians 4:22–23).

Stagnant periods
  may then become
    learning moments.
Entombed by defeat or loss,
  the stones may roll away
  and death be transformed
    into Life.
Surrounded by walls of water,
  you will walk with confidence
  in their midst
  to the Promised Land
    of peace.

Awesome Wonder

Second Sunday of Easter

(Acts 5:12–16; John 20:19–30)

A newborn baby is an awesome thing.
For an essentially helpless creature,
   a baby inspires
      amazing hopefulness,
   bringing an incredible
      sense of wonder to life.

Infants marvel at life's
   most mundane mysteries.
They notice everything—
   are fascinated
      by wrapping paper,
   entranced with
      colors and sounds,
   thrilled to laughter
      by a simple smile.

How did we adults lose
   this sense of wonder?

When did we forget
    what it was to be a child,
    forget that life in God, with God
    is meant to be awesome,
        wonder-full,
        grace-filled,
        miraculous.
How sad that the "grace of wonder"
    seems to diminish
    as life's skepticism and brutality
    touches us.
The author G. K. Chesterton wrote:
    "We have hands that fashion,
    and minds that know,
    but our hearts
        we have lost long ago."

Have you "lost your heart,"
    lost a sense of wonder,
    of awe at God's goodness?
Have you lost the ability
    to be stunned by grace,
    shocked by mercy,
    awed by majesty,
    as you have become
        busy and sophisticated
        in your "mature" adult lifestyle?

In the Old Testament,
    Yahweh-God caused people
    to fall to the ground in awe,
    to raise hands in praise,
    to even take one's shoes off
        when standing on holy ground.
The miracles of Jesus
    brought shouts of acclamation.

One stubborn, awestruck woman
    forced her way to Jesus—
convinced that only a
    touch of his garment
was needed for healing.
Even the apostle Thomas,
    when finally his skepticism
        melted away,
    could only cry out in wonder
        "My Lord and my God!"

Have you become
    a modern-day Thomas?
Would you demand
    to "put your hands in the wounds"
    before you believe what
    "eyes cannot see
        and ears cannot hear"?

Have you become so skeptical,
    so cynical, critical, and disparaging,
        about people,
    so suspicious, doubtful, and hardened
        about life,
    that you have lost the "grace of wonder"
    about our awesome God?

Have you lost
    that indescribable gratitude
    at what God has done
        in your life,
    at God's mercy,
        tenderness,
        care for you?

Have you lost the ability
    to be surprised by God,
    to receive a sudden onslaught
        of heavenly grace,
    to feel a spontaneous burst
        of divine joy,
    to be moved to tears
        by a Spirit-inspired word or song?

Do you ever cry out in prayer, as Thomas did,
    "My Lord and my God!"
    upon seeing the glory
        of the risen Lord?
Have you called out recently,
    "Hallelujah! Praise God!"
    in worship of the awesome majesty
        of his Presence?

Despite your cluttered, busy lifestyle,
    despite life hurts that have wounded
        your sense of awe,
    despite the skepticism
        of this modern world,
    never lose that sense
        of awesome wonder for your God.

Open your mind and heart once again
    to childlike awe,
    to gratitude and wonder
        at the glory of God's Name,
        and the power of God's Words.
Give your tongue
    permission to praise.
Allow your heart
    to be surprised by Joy
        once again!

Third Sunday of Easter

(John 21:1–14)

There is no more ancient job
   than that of fishing.
Countless millions throughout history,
   from every level of life,
   have fished for food, sport,
   entertainment, profession.
Hebert Hoover said that
   to really know someone,
   he had to take them fishing.

Experienced fishermen today
   target the general kind of fish
   they are looking for:
   trout, bass, muskie, walleye, etc.
The type of fish that people look for
   affects not only the bait used,
   but the places they go
   and the results they have.

The apostles in John 21,
   professional fishermen all,
   fished throughout the night

without catching a thing—
because they were fishing
   in the wrong places,
perhaps for the wrong thing
   at the wrong time.

But when they allowed Jesus
   to guide and lead them,
   to point out the way
   to the biggest fish
     of greatest value,
   their catch was overwhelming
   and profited them greatly.
"So they made a cast,
   and took in so many fish
   that they could not haul the net in" (John 21:7).

What are you "fishing for"
   in this world?
What fish are you
   "casting your nets" for
   in your everyday actions,
   by the plans you make,
   by your daily activities?
Everyone "fishes" for something in life.
   What are the goals and dreams,
   ambitions and hopes
   that drive your actions,
   and direct your daily routines?
What gets you out of bed each morning
   and keeps you going through the day?

Some people today "fish"
   for money, power, or success,
   for sexual or material pleasure,
   for happiness or personal fulfillment.

These are the "goals" that motivate,
    that impel and induce action.
Some are driven by love
    for family, spouse, or children;
    others by a mission or task
        or a vision of justice.
Still others wander aimlessly
    through life's long moments—
    unconscious of inner motivations,
    unaware of deep truths—
    "fishing" without purpose or plan.

Allow God to be the Guide
    for your "fishing trip"
    through this world.
Daily place before God
    all your plans and goals,
    your visions and dreams,
    your deepest needs and wants.
"Seek first the Kingdom of God,
    all other things
    will be given to you besides" (Matthew 6:33).

As you journey along
    the great fishing trip of life,
    work at allowing God to teach you
    the best places to "fish,"
    what kind of "fish" to catch,
        and even how to do it.
"I will instruct you and teach you
    in the way you should walk" (Psalm 32:8).

Allow God to lead you out
    into the "deep waters" of life—
    where the waters are rougher
        the personal challenges greater,
    but the catch is bigger, more valuable.

"A third time Jesus asked him,
'Simon, do you love me?'
Jesus told him, 'Feed my sheep . . .
follow me'" (John 21:17–19).

Crisis Planning

Fourth Sunday of Easter

(Acts 13:14, 43–52; John 10:27–30; Revelation 7:9, 14–17)

Crisis!
The word blares out daily
    from newspapers describing
    the latest world conflict.
The 1980s "gas crisis"
    was trumpeted worldwide
    as Middle East nations sought
    to raise oil prices.
Counselors use the word
    to capture crucial life stages—
    mid-life crisis,
    identity crisis.

However, crisis also
    is a very personal thing.
Every person on this planet
    at some point in life
    has to undergo their own
    personal crisis times.
Crisis may enter your life
    in many different ways:
    the death of a loved one,

the loss of a job,
    the betrayal of a friend—
but as surely as the rising sun,
know that it will visit you.

The question is not
    whether crisis will come,
    but rather, when it does come,
    how will you choose to confront it?
"The ultimate measure of a man
    is not where he stands
    in moments of comfort,
    but where he stands
    at times of challenge
        and controversy" (M. L. King).

To prepare for times of unrest,
    major cities have "crisis plans."
What is your personal "crisis plan"—
    the attitudes and actions
    you routinely fall back upon
    at moments of challenge and crisis?
It is the foundations built now,
    the spiritual "reactions" developed
        in times of peace and routine,
    that form the basis of how
    you instinctively respond in crisis.

Our Creator God knows crisis well,
    for he formed it and allows it
    to be the Potter's hand
    shaping the clay of our souls.
God offers three key insights
    to help form your personal
        "crisis plan."

"Jesus said, 'My sheep hear my voice.
    I know them, and they follow me'" (John 10:27).

Know who your true friends are,
    and who to listen to.
Many will offer advice and counsel
    when you face struggle or pain.
But true friends know your deep soul;
    they have courage to speak
        the gentle words,
        the challenging words,
        the wise words needed.
Deepen your relationship with
    the best Friend you have—
    the God who gave his life for you.

"A huge crowd stood before
    the throne and the Lamb:
    'these are the ones who
    have survived the great
        period of trial'" (Revelation 7:14).
Know well where you are going,
    and how best to get there.
Spend time evaluating your life goals—
    your meaning, purpose, destiny,
        in this world.
Constantly reassess in prayer
    the forces that drive you
    and the vision that leads you.
"Without a vision the people perish" (Proverbs 29:18).

"The Jews became very jealous,
    and countered with violent abuse . . .
The disciples knew only
    how to be filled with joy" (Acts 13:45, 52).
Held fast by friendship,
    your goals clear,
    have great courage (even boldness)
        in the face of resistance.

Walk forward into crisis
    guided by the light of your convictions,
    the courage of God's Presence within.
"Be not afraid, I am with you always" (Isaiah 43:5).

Crisis times are growth times.
Build strong foundations now,
    "and you shall never perish" (John 10:28).
"You will be led to springs
    of life-giving water,
    and God will wipe
    every tear from your eye" (Revelation 7:17).

Get Yourself Some Good Memories

Fifth Sunday of Easter

(Psalm 106; Acts 14:21–27)

"I will remember the deeds of the Lord" (Psalm 77:11).
One of the scourges of modern society
    are problems with dementia—
    especially Alzheimer's disease.

These are sicknesses of the mind,
    involving the loss of priceless pasts
    and precious years of memories.
They bring untold stress, loss, and pain
    to many families—
    including my own.

But perhaps a modern scourge
    of equal devastation today
    is "spiritual dementia"—
    a sickness of the soul
    where we forget God's
        innumerable blessings,
    and live in numbed insensitivity
        to the Spirit.

It seems to be an ageless problem.
In the Old Testament, one writer warns,
   "We have sinned, we and our fathers,
     we remembered not your abundant kindness.
   We soon forgot your works . . .
     forgot the God who had saved us" (Psalm 106:7–8).

What is behind this timeless human problem
   of "divine memory" retention?
Why is it that our minds so quickly forget
   what our God has done for us—
   those sweet movements of grace,
   the awesome concept
     of salvation for our sins,
   the unexpected blessings
     in our life?
Perhaps it is a problem of attitude:
   many are more focused on counting
   the curses of life
     instead of the blessings of faith.
Perhaps it is a problem of vision:
   it requires great openness of mind
   and rare flexibility of psyche
   to look beyond
     everyday mechanical routine
   and truly be open to seeing
     the sudden surprises of the Spirit.

Whatever the reason,
   a key part of a spiritual journey
   is the tireless combating of
     "spiritual dementia"—
   fighting forgetfulness
     and lack of gratitude,
   avoiding insensitivity
     to God's quiet movements.
We can do this in two ways.

First, we can cultivate
    an "attitude of gratitude"
    for all God has done in our life.
We can start each day with prayers of thanks—
    for personal blessings,
    for gentle unacknowledged graces,
    for people and things
        taken for granted.
"The favors of the Lord
    I will sing forever;
    through all generations
    my mouth will proclaim
        your faithfulness" (Psalm 89:2).

Second, we can get ourselves
    some "graced" memories—
    memories of the times people loved us
        when we did not expect it,
    times we found help
        from truly unexpected places,
    memories of a God who has been
        an ever present "Lord of History"
        through our entire life.
"On their arrival,
    they called the congregation together
    and related all that God
        had helped them accomplish,
    and how he had opened
        the door of faith
        to the Gentiles" (Acts 14:27).

Remembering the past with gratitude
    frees us
        for the present
    and encourages us
        in the future.
Remind yourself today that
    "everything works out for good."

Recall that Jesus taught his disciples to
  "Do this in memory of me."

Get yourself some good memories
  of God's blessings.
Stir up those memories
    into prayers of gratitude
      each and every day.
"I will remember the deeds of the Lord!" (Psalm 77:11)

The Spirit of Peace

Sixth Sunday of Easter

(John 14:23–29)

Farewells are always hard.
Saying goodbye to a loved one,
    leaving some special idyllic place,
    parting painfully at moments of death:
    all of these leave a strange hollowness,
      an empty loneliness,
      in one's soul.

As Jesus of Nazareth left this world,
    he knew all too well his own disciples
    would be lonely and lost,
      often overwhelmed
    by the world around them
    and the task he had for them.

Thus before his death,
    this great Teacher and Prophet
    spoke powerful words of great significance:

"Do not be distressed . . .
   do not be afraid.
You have heard me say
   that I was going away for a while,
   and I will come back to you" (John 14:27–28).

Jesus Christ had long warned his followers
   that he would not physically remain with them forever,
   that he had to return to his Father's home—
      just as we would one day
      be called to do as well.
But in his unique divine wisdom,
   Jesus wisely left something behind,
   giving his followers a farewell present—
   a gift of Power, Peace, and Presence
      called "Spirit."

"This much have I told you
   while I was still with you;
   the Paraclete, the Holy Spirit,
   will instruct you in everything,
   and remind you of all I told you" (John 14:25–26).

This Gift was far more
   than a farewell memento,
   the promised Spirit
      was an awesome power—
   a power of the Love
      between Father and Son,
   a power of Truth
      that would energize and enable,
   a power that burst forth on Pentecost
      taking men and women
         out of fear and isolation
         into freedom, boldness, and faith.

"It is much better for you that I go.
If I fail to go,
  the Spirit will never come . . .
when he comes,
  being the Spirit of Truth,
you will be guided
  into all truth" (John 16:7,13).

Today, strangely enough,
  the Master's farewell gift
  remains one of the most ignored tools
  in the average Christian's
    arsenal of faith resources.
It is vital for our life and faith
  that we learn to release
  the "farewell gift"—
  the Spirit of power and peace,
    that our Teacher left us.

God's Spirit is a motivating Power,
  an energizing Force
  that can push away
  the deepest of apathies and fears.
Take strength from the Spirit of Power.

God's Spirit is that gentle touch of Peace
  in the midst of anxiety and stress,
  a calming energy flowing through you,
  restoring health and life.
Rest in the Spirit of Peace.

God's Spirit is a consoling Presence
  in times of aloneness,
  a gentle Compassion
  in life's most fearsome times.
Know you are never alone
  in the Spirit of God.

"Fan into flame
the gift God gave you . . .
you have not received
a spirit of fear
but of power!" (2 Timothy 1:6)

Getting Personal with God

Seventh Sunday of Easter

(Acts 7:55–60; John 17:20–26; Revelation 22:12–20)

When we allow ourselves to be loved
   by some special person,
   it is an amazing thing.
We allow the beloved
   to get close to us,
   to share intimate parts of self,
   to "get personal" with our heart
   in ways
   few are ever allowed to do.

Our great and awesome God
   is a Being far above ourselves
   in wisdom, understanding,
      power, and love.
We cannot begin to comprehend
   even the remotest fraction
      of this infinite, immense cosmic Reality.
Yet the utterly amazing truth about God
   is that this unfathomable Being
   throughout history
   desires to "get personal"
      with his creation.

Our astonishing God has always chosen
   to get deeply involved,
      even obsessed
   in every aspect of human lives.
More than that,
   our infinite Supreme Being
   continually reveals himself to us
      as an immensely personal
      and passionate God.
"Father to them
   I have revealed your name . . .
   so that your love for me
      may live in them,
   and I may live in them" (John 17:26).

Jesus was passionate
   with those he loved.
He ate dinners with Martha and Mary
   and raised his friend Lazarus
      from the dead.
He stirred up Matthew, Peter, and others
   by calling them to be
   more than they ever imagined
      they could be.
He shed tears over a city he loved,
   which had rejected him
      and his words.
His last earthly words were a prayer
   that his companions
      would be with him forever.
"Father, all those you gave me,
   I would have in my company,
   to see this glory of mine" (John 17:24).

God has always been more than willing
   to get involved
   in our messes and mishaps—
   indeed this is why Jesus died for us.

"God so loved the world
that he gave his only Son" (John 3:16).

What God brings to a relationship is vast—
  comfort in loneliness,
    compassion in brokenness,
  healing for wounds,
    food for the spirit,
  forgiveness for sins,
    salvation for your soul.
"We do not have a God
  unable to sympathize with us,
  but one who was tempted
    in every way we are" (Hebrews 3:15).

God is committed to getting personal
  with every aspect of your life—
  but only when he is invited to do so.
God will become as intimate with you
  as you allow and invite God to be.

Is your relationship with God
  as deeply personal and passionate
    as God has been with you?
Do you share a personal friendship
  with the God who gave you life,
    or is yours
    a distant, detached "agreement"
  with a formal and impersonal Deity?
"Not everyone that cries 'Lord, Lord'
  will enter the Kingdom of heaven" (Matthew 7:21).

Do you long for God's presence,
  look for God's movements,
  love God more than life itself?
Are you determined to follow him
  wherever the road leads?
Are you determined not to be discouraged,

to "never be weary
of doing good"?
Are you willing to be
detained by God—
to follow God's inexplicable
ways and detours
in every part of your life,
your relationships and work?
Are you willing
to have your life changed,
molded "as clay
in the hands of the potter"?

Become as personal
with your God,
as passionate
with your Creator
as your God
has been with you.
"Lord Jesus, receive my spirit!" (Acts 7:59)

Forgotten and Overlooked

Pentecost

(Acts 2:1–11 ; John 20:19–23

For years, Rodney Dangerfield
  has built his comic career
  on the phrase
  "I don't get no respect."
Everyone remembers
  the great accomplishments
  of athletes like Michael Jordan,
    Mark McGuire,
    or Tiger Woods;
  but few remember
    their teammates or runners-up.
There are so many forgotten ones
  in our world today—
  people who seem to never get
  the respect, notice, or appreciation
  they truly deserve.

But did you know that even God
    has this problem?
There are three Persons
  comprising that marvelous
  Mystery of Magnificence

that is our God, yet one
    seems to be a missing Person.
The forgotten and overlooked
    eternal resident of heaven
        is the Spirit of God.
"We have not so much as heard
    that there is a Holy Spirit" (Acts 19:2).

Passing liturgical church prayers
    do acknowledge the Spirit's reality,
    but images of "flying doves"
        often float through believers' minds.
Most have relegated the Spirit
    to a passive decoration
    on the dusty faith-shelf of life.
For many generations,
    this powerful Spirit of God
    was known by the word *Ghost*—
    which one dictionary defines
        as a "disembodied human spirit,
        usually harmful or evil."

Allow me to assure you
    that all this is *not* who God is!

The powerful Spirit of Pentecost
    is not a ghost
    nor a flying bird
    nor a forgotten phrase
        in church prayers.
The Spirit of the living God
    is a dynamic, living reality—
    alive, active, and very real
        in this and every generation.
"All were filled with the Holy Spirit . . .
    and began to make bold proclamations" (Acts 2:4).

The awesome Holy Spirit
   is an emphasizing Energy
      transforming all it touches,
   a liberating Power
      unleashed by active faith
      turning one's life upside down.
"Each one heard these men
   speaking their own language.
   The whole occurrence astonished them" (Acts 2:6–7).

The Spirit of God
   is the passion and fire,
   the intimacy and awesome Love
   that inflames and defines
   not only the relationship of
      Abba Father and Jesus the Son
   but also the relationship
      between ourselves and our God.
"God is love.
   Whoever lives in love
   lives in God,
   and God in him.
   In this way,
   love is made perfect" (1 John 4:16–17).

If you have the courage to do it,
   let go of your urge
      to control and structure
      all of your faith life
   and let loose the Energy,
      passion, and fire
      of the Spirit of God!
Allow your faith to be
   emboldened,
   stretched,
   empowered
   by the

uncontrollable,
unquenchable fire
of Energy and Love
that is Spirit!

Come alive in Spirit-peace!
"The Holy Spirit will instruct you . . .
Peace is my farewell to you,
my peace is my gift to you" (John 14:27).

Come alive in Spirit-power!
"You will receive Power
when the Holy Spirit comes upon you" (Acts 1:8).

Come alive in divine wisdom!
"Do not worry about
how to defend yourself . . .
the Holy Spirit will
teach you at that time
what you are to say" (Luke 12:12).

Lifting the Veil of Heaven

Trinity Sunday

(Deuteronomy 4:32–40; Romans 8:14–17; Matthew 28:16–20)

Occasionally ecstasy happens.
Amidst the dull routine of life
    something occurs that is truly
    an overpowering moment
        of happiness,
    an ecstatic moment
        of one-ness or joy.
Perhaps a moment between lovers,
    a sunset of grandeur,
    a powerful prayer time.
It is as if
for the briefest of moments
    a corner of the veil
    between heaven and earth is lifted—
and we glimpse
    in a flickering flash
    the absolute joy
        of what lies ahead.

Such all-too-rare experiences
    pull us out of this
        limited plane of existence

into an eternal world
 of unexplainable Mystery,
 of Passion beyond emotion,
 of Oneness with the One.
We can continue to touch
 that World of wonder,
 that *mysterium tremendum* that is God,
 by developing a personal relationship
  (an intimate oneness
  of mind and spirit)
 with each of the Persons
 of that World:
  the Creator Father,
  the Savior Son Jesus,
  the Energizing Spirit.

You were brought into this world,
 created and "loved into life"
 by a God we aptly call "Father"—
 a God who "holds you
  in the palm of his hand,"
 who made you "a little less
  than the angels,"
 in "his own image and likeness."
This Person has the
 strength, courage, and power
  of a Father (an *Abba*),
 the compassion, wisdom, and fortitude
  of a Mother (an *Ema*).
The Creator is for you, both
 a life-anchoring *Abba*,
 and an angst-soothing *Ema*.

You were redeemed and saved,
 truly set free
  from sin, lust, and pride
 by a God we know as *Jeshua*—
Jesus Christ from Nazareth,

the Anointed One
who "suffered in every way we did,"
who "became one of us, even unto death,"
who is the Light of our world—
    our Way, Truth, and Life.
This Person
    is a Brother and a Friend,
    indeed he *"walks with me,*
    and he talks with me,
    and he tells me I am his own."

You are empowered and energized
    by the God we call "Spirit"—
the One who
    "guides you to all truth,"
the One who
    gives you every "good gift
    from above,"
the One who
    gifts you with "words and wisdom
    when you need them."
This Person energizes the depths
    of your fear and uncertainty.
"For we did not receive
    a spirit of slavery
    leading us back into fear,
    but a Spirit of adoption
    through which we cry out
    'Abba'" (Romans 8:15).

Praise God for these Three!
They lift the veil of heaven
    as we walk through
    the vales of earth.
They tantalize us
    with earthly glimpses
    of heavenly Glory,
    of Ecstasy to come!

Praise God today that you are
    "heirs of God,
    heirs with Christ,
    if only we suffer with him" (Romans 8:17).
Enjoy those rare moments
    of heavenly ecstasy here—
    but prepare yourself
    to be worthy for the
        "lifting of the veil."

"Know that I
    am with you always
    until the end of time" (Matthew 28:20).

Hungers of the Heart

Corpus Christi

(1 Corinthians 11:23–26; Luke 9:11–17)

On a particularly long hiking trip
    many years ago,
    our food supply
      ran very low.
By the sixth and last night
    in the wilderness,
    our entire "dinner" for four
    consisted of
    two small freeze-dried packages of eggs.
I experienced that night,
    for the first time in my life,
    true hunger.

Some people in this world
    hunger daily and desperately
    for physical bread and food.
Most of us in the Western world
    have never experienced
      this level of need,
    but perhaps our unique hungers are worse.

Our deepest hungers are usually not
    for food, shelter, or clothing—
    but are hungers
        of the human heart.
These yearnings are not easily filled—
    7-11 and Walmart
        do not satisfy here.

We hunger for fulfillment in our lives,
    happiness in our relationships,
    safety for our children,
    peace in the midst
        of pain and problems.
Some crave success, prosperity, and pleasure—
    the sating of satisfied sensuality,
    the numbing of intense loneliness,
    the meaning of a purpose for one's life.

Today, God reminds us of a simple truth—
    this world's pleasures
        will always leave us
    hungry, unfulfilled, and incomplete.
Jesus once said it best
    as he spoke at a well
    with a truly "thirsting" woman:
"Everyone who drinks this water
    will be thirsty again.
But whoever drinks the water I give
    will never be thirsty" (John 4:13–14).

In truth, the hungers of the human heart
    can only be satisfied
        with food for the soul:
    with the solid "bread"
        of God's words and wisdom,
    and the "waters"
        of Life, healing, and peace.

It is only *"the hand of the Lord*
that feeds us,
and God that answers
all our needs" (Psalm 145:16).

God's Word fills that
"hole in our soul,"
planting objective and purpose there,
giving direction and meaning
to the rootless wanderings
of the human spirit.
"In he who is my strength,
I have strength for everything" (Philippians 4:13).

God's compassion and mercy
soothe the soul,
easing the guilt of sin
and personal weakness,
softening stubborn spirits
with forgiveness, hope, and renewal.
"Come and see the man
who told me everything I did!
Could this not be the Messiah?" (John 4:29)

God's firm yet gentle teachings
guide the soul,
and the discipline of his laws
provides guidance to the wayward,
instruction for the unenlightened,
teaching for seeking spirits.
"Happy the person who delights
in the law of the Lord . . .
whatever he does prospers" (Psalm 1:2).

God's touch heals
   the anxious hungers in our heart,
   dispelling dark yearnings
     that rise unbidden,
   scattering the needy fears
     that life brings upon us.
"Know that I am with you always,
   even until
     the end of the world!" (Matthew 28:20)

Barrier-Breaking

Twelfth Sunday in Ordinary Time

(Galatians 3:26–29)

"There does not exist among you
Jew or Greek,
slave or free,
rich or poor" (Galatians 3:28).
And yet sadly, there does.

In every country of the world,
    every neighborhood of our cities
    (in our churches as well),
    in every person's heart,
    there exists division and separation.
For some it may best be called intolerance,
    for others, prejudice or prejudgment,
    perhaps classism or favoritism.

Other descriptions for this curious flaw
    in primal human nature
    might be discrimination, hypocrisy, bias—
    or worst, racism and bigotry.

However described,
    there exists in the human heart
    a brokenness and woundedness
    tearing apart the unity
        God created us for.
It is part of the "original sin,"
    the broken human condition
    we have been born into:
    "in sin my mother conceived me" (Psalm 51:7).
"What happens is that I do
    not the good I will to do,
    but the evil I do not intend" (Romans 7:19).

We may profess to abhor racism personally,
    yet subtly continue and condone it
    by our jokes and language,
    or by our neighborhood housing choices.

We profess love for peace and harmony,
    yet are quick to rejoice
        in military actions
    that preserve our precious
        oil supply.
We may profess scandal at divisions
    between church denominations,
    yet do not find time to worship
    with a believer
        of another tradition.
We may profess personal love
    of God and neighbor,
    yet find ourselves stubbornly enmeshed
    in office feuds
        and grudge-holding.

In God, there are no barriers at all.
There are no walls between the Persons
    comprising our Infinite God.

All is one, whole,
  united, indivisible.
"The Father and I are one" (John 10:30).

Jesus' last prayer for humanity was
  "Father may they be one . . . " (John 17:11)
His desire was that our sundered spirits
  might again be reunited,
  all human barriers broken down—
  echoing the heavenly Union
    awaiting us.
*"There does not exist among you
  Jew or Greek, male or female . . . "* (Galatians 3:28)

Unity is possible in our human condition—
  when people share common values
  of deep, personal conviction.
Ancient barriers can be torn down—
  when the Power that unites
  is greater than
  the forces that divide.

Allow your passion for God
  to become a conscious, daily choice
  for unity, dialogue,
    and barrier-breaking.
Begin confronting the denial and fear,
  ignorance and anxiety,
  underpinning all prejudice
    and prejudgment.
Daily pray for the Spirit
  of Truth and Courage
  to surround your personal "walls"
  (racial, psychological, cultural)
    and slowly begin
    to dismantle them.

"Create a clean heart in me, O God,
   and a steadfast spirit
      renew in me" (Psalm 51:10).

Pray to be "oned" in your heart—
   oned to the God who is All in All,
   oned to his creation around you.
Open your mind to search out
   any barriers, walls, prejudices,
   that hold you back from this goal
   of Oneness with the One.

There are no earthly limitations
   when God's Power is active and alive.
"All things are possible
   for those who love God."

No human barriers are insurmountable
   when people are in God's Spirit.
"Every one of you is
   a son or daughter of God" (Galatians 3:26).

Thirteenth Sunday in Ordinary Time

(Galatians 5:1, 13–18; John 8:32)

Independence and freedom.
In these two simple words
　　lie more misunderstanding
　　　　and self-deception
　　than any other words
　　　　in our American heritage.
"I gotta do my own thing."
　　"No one tells me what to do."
　　"It's my body, I can do with it what I want."

These deceptive definitions of "freedom"
　　are echoed constantly
　　　　in modern culture.
America is somehow
　　supposed to be all about
　　these superficial, self-centered clichés,
　　which some mistakenly think
　　　　are even "inalienably guaranteed."

Yet God's Word, too,
　　has a "philosophy" of freedom:

"You have been called
to live in freedom—
but not a freedom that gives
free reign to the flesh" (Galatians 5:13).
God's definition of human "freedom"
    differs vastly from the trite truisms
    heard so often
        on modern talk shows.
True freedom does *not* mean
    freedom to do whatever we want,
    freedom from anyone telling us what to do,
    freedom to carry a weapon or abort a child,
    freedom from obligations,
        commitments, or responsibility.
Ironically, these "freedoms"
    only make us slaves—
    to extremism, intolerance, bigotry,
    to passion, lust, pride, and ego.

Real freedom is paradoxical:
    it is rooted outside ourselves,
    far surpassing mere
        freedom from restraints.

Real freedom springs from
    commitment to higher purposes—
    from commitment
        to the greatest Truth of all:
"You shall know the Truth,
and the Truth will set you free" (John 8:32).

Real freedom is found
    in unselfish service
    of our fellow human beings:
"Out of love, place yourselves
at one another's service" (Galatians 5:14).

Real freedom is being rooted in God,
   finding our identity in being
      God's beloved son or daughter;
   and then (in response to that Love)
   reaching out of ourselves in service
      to the world, to others, to our God.

When we find the inner freedom and peace
   that comes only from God's Presence within,
   we do not have need
      to act out or show off—
   we become freed *from*
      to be free *for!*
Free *from* self, ego, and lust,
   to be free *for* others:
      for service,
      for lifelong commitment.
"It was for liberty
   that Christ freed us,
   so do not take on yourself
   the yoke of slavery
      a second time!" (Galatians 5:1)

Work at becoming truly free
   in every area of your being.
Begin to move past shallow freedoms,
   past self-gratifying
      definitions of freedom
   foisted on you by media and others.
True inner freedom does not lie
   in being beyond any authority,
   outside any control,
   having no boundaries or limitations.

True freedom lies paradoxically in commitment:
   in commitment to God
      you will find your truest Self,
   in commitment to another
      you will find deep, honest Love,
   and in feeding the sick,
      clothing the hungry,
      working for justice—
   you will find the doorway to heaven.

"Choose this day who you will serve . . .
as for me and my house,
we will serve the Lord" (Joshua 24:15).

Your Most Valuable Possession

Fourteenth Sunday in Ordinary Time

(Philippians 4:30; Luke 10:17–20; Revelation 3:5, 20:12)

What is
    your most valuable possession—
    the one item beyond price
    guaranteeing your
        eternal worth and value?
What is the one item
    that cannot be stolen or taken—
    but which can be ruined and degraded?
It is your name—
    your unique, highly personal
        good name.
A person's name
    is one's exclusive identity,
        a matchless legacy,
        divinely bequethed
        both in time
        and in eternity.

From the first day
    of earthly existence,
    your name is recorded endlessly
        in countless places:

from courtrooms
    to classrooms,
from legal records
    to paychecks.
Where you consciously choose
    to place or sign your unique name
    marks out who you are
    both in this world
    and the next.
Where your name is,
    there are reflected
    your life decisions,
    your personal endorsements,
    your bond of commitments,
    your promises of support,
    your sponsorship,
        your very self.

In the Bible,
    when a name was given or changed,
    it denoted a special status or call:
    Abram became Abraham,
        "father of nations";
    Simon became Peter,
        "rock" of the Church;
    Saul became Paul,
        evangelist, writer, and preacher.

In the end, there is only one place
    where it desperately matters
    that your name be written:
    in the book that is
    Life eternal.
"Do not rejoice because
    the spirits are subject to you,
    but rejoice because
    your names are being written
    in heaven" (Luke 10:20).

Your name gets written
    in the Book of Life
    only by the life choices you make—
       and most importantly,
    by a conscious fundamental option
    for God to become
       the center of your life,
       the axis of all your actions.
"Most important is this:
    love the Lord your God
    with all your heart,
       all your soul,
       all your mind,
       all your strength" (Mark 12:29).

You then engrave your name eternally
    by intentional actions
       of love and kindness
    faithfully done
       during your sojourn on earth—
    actions done unselfishly
       for others,
    actions that heal,
       encourage,
       elevate Life.
"The second is this:
    love your neighbor
       as yourself" (Mark 12:31).

There is one Name
    above all other names—
    a Name of power, peace, and Presence,
    the mere speaking of which
       invokes blessing and authority.
Use well this name,
    and use it often—
    the sweet name
       of Jesus.

Always be wise and careful
  about how you wield
  the gift of your unique name.
Use your name
  to make fundamental life choices
  for hope, love, and compassion.
Be careful not to misuse it
  or even abuse it—
  because where you sign your name
  you sign your very self.

"The victor will be dressed in white,
and I will never erase his name
from the book of life" (Revelation 3:5).

Inconvenient Love

Fifteenth Sunday in Ordinary Time

(Deuteronomy 30:10–14; Luke 10:25–36)

Opportunities to do good for someone
   rarely ever come
     at convenient times.
It is strange but true
   that people or situations
     crying for help
   always seem to occur
     when we are busy already,
   when our "plate is full"
     of commitments,
   when we are on our way
     to something else.

Such opportunities to do something "good"
   involve an inevitable,
   critical moment of choice:
   "Do I stop my own busy life to help,
     assisting however I can,
   or go on about my business
     trusting that someone else
     will come along?"

"Do I risk getting involved
with something
that could considerably change my schedule,
   perhaps drawing me in
   far deeper than expected—
or do I allow myself,
   and consciously choose,
to become inconvenienced for Love?"

These critical moments of choice in life
   present themselves often
      to every person.

The priest and temple attendant of Luke 10
   were important and busy people;—
   both were committed "church people,"
   dedicated to God's work professionally.
But when that critical moment came upon them,
   they couldn't risk
      being inconvenienced—
   they wouldn't change
      their busy lifestyles,
      their self-important commitments,
   by stopping to help a wounded man.

Curiously, it was a sworn ancestral enemy
   who found time to not only stop,
   but to provide follow-up care,
      even financial payment
   after leaving the "scene of the crime"!

This sworn enemy took time
   to "get involved."
He went beyond "ordinary love,"
   stopping not just for immediate help—
   but inconveniencing himself
   by pouring oil on the wounds,
      putting the man on his beast,
      bringing him to an inn,
      returning several days later
      to pay the bill!

True Christian love is choosing
   to be inconvenienced
   for one of God's people.
It is love beyond the "call of duty,"
   "even to death, death on the cross."
God's command to us on earth
   "is not too mysterious or remote—
   it is something very near you,
   already in your mouths and hearts—
      you only have to carry it out"
      (Deuteronomy 30:13–14).

Sometimes we make God's ways
   far too complex—
   after committing our life to God,
   the second divine demand
   is disturbingly simple:
inconvenient love,
being willing to be inconvenienced
   for another human person.

"Love the Lord your God
with all your heart, soul,
mind, strength;
love your neighbor
as yourself" (Luke 10:27).

It is a love
    that takes you "out of your way"
    to help bring another
        into God's way.
It is a complete and unselfish love
    that allows,
        indeed, consciously chooses,
    to put another's concerns
        above your own.
It is love above and beyond
    the call of duty—
    just like the love your God had
    when he inconvenienced himself for you
        by dying on the cross.

"'Which of these in your opinion,
    was neighbor?'
The answer came,
    'The one who treated him
    with compassion.'
Jesus said to him,
    'Then go out
    and do likewise'" (Luke 10:36–37).

Too Busy for God?

Sixteenth Sunday in Ordinary Time

(Luke 10:38–42)

Martha has been a victim
    of bad press.
While Mary sat at Jesus' feet,
    Martha's bustling around the house
        (her "work ethic," so to speak—
        a truly "American" one, by the way)
    has been chided and castigated.
Even Jesus said she was
    "busy about many things,
    when only one thing was needed" (Luke 10:41).
Pseudo-contemplatives
    have made her active work style
    a whipping post.

But there was nothing bad
    in what she did!
Martha was illustrating
    love of one's neighbor.
She fulfilled Paul's later dictum:
    "Unless a person works,
        he should not eat" (2 Thessalonians 3:10).

Martha's work ethic (in general)
   was not being criticized!

What Jesus did say here
   was that
   in *this* circumstance,
   with *these* specific guests,
     Mary had chosen the *better* part.
So there was nothing bad
   about Martha's role;
   it was simply that
   her sister made
     a wiser choice!

Because on that great day
   Jesus was their guest.
   He was "in the house."
The Lord and Master,
   Son of David and Son of God,
   the Galilean miracle worker
   was sharing their home and hearth.
Mary chose to be fully present to Greatness,
   to sit quietly at his feet,
   to drink deeply of
     his wisdom and grace.

At that moment, in that small space,
   in that unique moment
     in their life history,
   this was a wiser choice.
It was a better use
   of the very limited time
   these two special friends of Jesus
   had to spend
   with their divine friend
     who would soon leave them
     to give his life for them.

The story teaches the need
  of a balanced life—
  of working hard and well
  with one's God-given talents and gifts;
  but also of praying sincerely
    in a focused, committed way
    to energize the work one does.

Martha's mistake is one most of us make;
  it is one of balance—
  of not keeping the urgently important
  forces of life
    such as work, prayer, family, ministry,
  in proper equilibrium
    and perspective.

Knowing when to be busy,
  when to work—and work hard,
  when to love—and be loved,
but knowing when to stop
    ceaseless activity,
  when to shut off
    the noise of the day,
  when to sit in silence
    before the Silent One,
  when to quiet oneself and pray deeply
    to the God
    who is beyond time and work:
this is the key to life-balance.

Is your life in balance?

Are you "busy about many things
  when only one thing is required"?

Work for a sense of proportion in your life,
   a "right order"
      between family and career,
   solitude with self
      and presence to others,
   God-consciousness
      and world-consciousness.
If you are too busy
   to be in balance,
   too busy to pray—
   then you simply
      are too busy.

As Paul says,
   "Put on a new way of thinking":
   a healthy harmony
   of going "in" to seek the Lord
      in your deepest soul-recesses,
   but then going back "out"
      to be of service
      to our world.

The Greatest Prayer

Seventeenth Sunday in Ordinary Time

(Luke 11:1–13)

Our Father who are in heaven . . .

God, you are to me
    Father and Mother.
I place myself
    into your hands
    completely.
"Into your hands O Lord,
    I commend my spirit" (Luke 23:46).

Holy is your name . . .

The name of Jesus—
    what a precious thing!
"Every knee shall bow,
    every tongue confess
    the name of Jesus as Lord" (Philippians 2:10).
How often is your name
    misused, abused today—
    may your name be praised!

Your kingdom come, your will be done . . .

Not *my* kingdom Lord—*your* Kingdom.
Your Kingdom is a Kingdom of peace,
   of healing, of forgiveness,
   of transformation, of courage, of boldness.
Human kingdoms are about
   control, power, glory, pleasure.
I yield my kingdoms
   to your greatest Kingdom;
   I yield my plans, projects, worries, to you.
"Your will be done."

On earth as it is in heaven . . .

Salvation is not reserved for heaven;
   it is for earth as well.
"With the Lord is
   the fullness of redemption" (Psalm 130:7).
Give me that deep inner peace
   here and now, Lord,
   wherever I am hurting and lonely,
   dejected, afraid, and lost.
Heal me as I struggle
   on this earth today.

Give us this day our daily bread . . .

Lord, I get so overwhelmed at times,
   overworked, truly stressed out.
Help me to take life
   one day at a time.
I want the whole loaf of bread,
   but you remind me to ask
   for only one slice a day,
   "our daily bread."

Help me live one day at a time,
    one hour at a time,
    one minute at a time, if need be.

Forgive us our sins
as we forgive those who sin against us . . .

This is where faith gets hard.
I know that I stand in need
    of your mercy;
    I am aware of my weakness and sin,
    my failures and brokenness.
But here you remind me
    that *your* forgiveness
    is tied to *my* forgiveness
        of others in my life.
Lord, help me to acknowledge
    my own need for forgiveness—
    my resentment, bitterness, anger.
Show me where I need to "unbind,"
    to forgive others or self.

Lead us not into temptation . . .

Lord, I always seem to be
    in the middle of temptation.
I am tempted many ways:
        to give up hope,
        to become blasé,
        to just "doing my job"
        to being self-centered,
        to lashing out at people,
        to getting even.
Lord, walk with me through temptation.
You were there,
    you know what it was like;
    you know our humanness.

But deliver us from evil . . .

Evil is real,
   not a figment of my imagination.
Evil is very real and very alive—
   evils of drugs and gangs,
   of abuse both physical and addictive,
   of crime, racism, and prejudice,
   of personal hypocrisy and self-righteousness,
   of being a "frozen chosen"
      (without hope, joy,
     or the power of the Spirit).
Free me from those evils by your Power.

So my gentle Lord and powerful Savior,
   I end up back where I started:
   "Our Father."
   I am completely
     in your hands.
   All that I do today
   I consciously choose to do
   for your greater honor and glory.

"Into your hands O Lord,
   I commend my spirit" (Luke 23:46).

WEEK 38

Greed

Eighteenth Sunday in Ordinary Time

(Ecclesiastes 1:2, 2:21–23; Colossians 3:1–5, 9–11; Luke 12:13–21)

*"Avoid greed
in all its forms"* (Luke 12:15).
Frank Munzie was a publisher—
a millionaire who owned
four houses around the world,
fully staffed at all times.
He had already planned
for his own lavish funeral—
but when he died,
not one mourner came.
He had been so busy
making money, traveling,
that he had no time
for friends,
or for God.

"Avoid greed in all its forms."
Greed is grasping for things,
an excessive desiring or lusting
to possess some thing—
an object, a person,

or even an abstract concept.
It is often paraded as virtue
   in modern America.
   "Greed is a good thing."
   "Grab all you can—
      you only go around once!"

People consider it normal
   that smooth businessmen
      lust after their next purchase,
   that immature athletes
      sate themselves with whatever they crave,
   that many Americans
      spend more and more
      on bigger and bigger items
      that are less and less important.

But Jesus says something today
   that shocks and challenges
   any serious soul-seeker:
   "Whatever a person possesses
   does not guarantee him life" (Luke 12:16).
Merely having money or wealth,
   or possessing many "things"
   is not the problem;
   it is the influence they play,
   the inflated importance they assume,
   the spoiled self-indulgence some have
      which is the issue.

Jesus was never against money,
   only the effect it has on people.
"Vanity of vanities!
   All things are vanity!" (Ecclesiastes 1:2)

We need to learn the difference
   between legitimate needs
   and excessive desires.

Humans need certain basic things
    to function in this world,
    and, indeed, have a right to them:
    food, job, housing,
    basic relationships,
    enough money to live on.
But when our desires
    begin to control *us*—
    when there are few limits,
    and little self-control—
    it is then that warning bells
    should sound in our spirit.

"What does it profit a person
    to gain the world
    but lose his soul?" (Matthew 16:26)
Never let any earthly thing,
    any human lust or appetite,
    any one person in life
    control or dominate you—
        not food, sex, or wealth,
        not personal security or power,
        not a spouse, friend, or job.
Allow only One to be in control
    of your life and your desires—
    the Creator God
        who loved you to life,
    and in whose arms
        you can fall in utter safety.

"Set your heart on what pertains
    to the higher realms . . .
    be intent on things above
    rather than on things of earth" (Colossians 3:1–2).
Live your life by reference points
    greater than yourself,
    beyond your own human desires.

Only there will you find
   the inner peace
   passing mere human understanding.
Let God be the still point of life—
   the Rock by which you judge
   the true value of all things.

While you walk in this world,
   live in peace
   and work for justice.
Seek true wealth
   by falling into your God.
"Seek first the Kingdom of God,
   and all things will
   be given you besides" (Matthew 6:33).

WEEK 39

Faith to Face the Future

Nineteenth Sunday in Ordinary Time

(Hebrews 11:1–2, 8–19; Luke 12:32–48)

An Englishman visited a friend
    in the depths of Africa,
    and was invited
        to go hunting with him.
When they came upon a lion's tracks,
    the African started to follow
    but the timid Englishman said,
    "You go ahead and see
        where he went—
    I'll go back and see
        where he came from!"

Religion is filled with timid people—
    people afraid to be
        bold and confident;
    people more interested
        in preserving the past
        than moving boldly into the future;
    people so worried about the present,
        they obsess about the "horrible future."

But Scripture says:
"Faith is confident assurance
concerning what we hope for,
and conviction about
    things we do not see" (Hebrews 11:1).

Faith is the key
    to confident,
    even enthusiastic living
    in both the present and future.
Not the static faith of religious dogma,
    or mere adherence
        to orthodox legalism,
    or absolute intellectual creeds
        and well-defined doctrines—
    for faith is not mere fundamentalist reliance
        on a rigid blanket of beliefs.
"A person is not justified
    by works of the law
    but through faith
        in Jesus Christ" (Galatians 2:16).

Our model is rather the living faith
    of Jesus the Master—
        supple yet strong,
        flexible yet firm,
    a lifestyle of Spirit-inspired assurance,
    an attitude of Father-conscious conviction.
Living faith
    is assurance prompting action
        in the present;
    conviction spurring confidence
        in the future.
"Do not live in fear, little flock.
    It has pleased your Father
        to give you the Kingdom!" (Luke 12:32)

Confident faith
  is an inner attitude:
  "In all things
  God works for the good
    of those who love him" (Romans 8:28).
Confident assurance
  is living by the creed:
  "We walk by faith
    not by sight" (2 Corinthians 5:7).

Abraham is an example
  of "confident assurance."
"By faith he obeyed when he was called,
  he went forth without knowing
    where he was going" (Hebrews 11:8).
When commanded to sacrifice his only son,
  he walked fearlessly forward;
  as a result,
  "His descendants were as numerous
    as sand on the shore,
    as stars in the sky" (Hebrews 11:12).

Live your entire life
  (past, present, and future)
  from this framework of "living faith."
Look into your past
  and rejoice in the accomplishments
    God has allowed you,
  for in past rememberings
  courage is gained
    for the future.

Trust God completely in the present moment.
Know that nothing will happen today
  that you and God cannot handle—
  because *"I am with you always"* (Matthew 28:20).

Face your future with Power,
with confidence and conviction,
assurance and certitude—
because *"Where else can I go?*
You have the words of eternal life.
We have come to believe . . . " (John 6:68–69)

"Faith is confident assurance
about what we hope for,
conviction about what we do not see" (Hebrews 11:1).

"Let the fire fall . . ."

Twentieth Sunday in Ordinary Time

(Luke 12:49–53)

Revolution and revolt,
   radical upheaval and change,
   fire consuming everything:
   can this be our God speaking?
Such concepts are not usually associated
   with Jesus Christ, called often
   the "Prince of Peace,"
   the "lamb led to the slaughter."

Yet the words of Luke today
   are a challenging call
   to radical changes in life.
Jesus Christ was not just about
   giving "warm fuzzies" to people.
Following his call is about
   total personal transformation,
   complete spiritual revolution.
"I have come to light a fire on the earth.
   How I wish the blaze were ignited!
   Do you think I have come for peace?
   The contrary is true—
      I have come for division" (Luke 12:49–51).

Jesus Christ did indeed come
   to light a fire on earth—
   not a fire of terror or fear,
   but a fire of the Word of God
      moving and shaping,
      molding and transforming
   not only individual people's lives
   but also our entire human culture.
"For our God is a consuming fire."

Fire destroys and engulfs everything.
Fire can cause pain and division.
   It is this that makes
   the message of the Master
   hard to hear for many people.
Jesus consciously intends to bring
   the divine fire of transformation
   first and foremost
   within our own hearts.

It is always a horrendous struggle
   to yield up control of our humanity—
      wayward thoughts and actions,
      stubborn plans and egos,
      rebellious desires and lusts—
   to the Higher Power of God's grace.
Our human psyche fiercely resists
   the radical personal reshaping
   of values, goals, plans, and actions
   that the fire of God's Spirit brings.

As you struggle to allow yourself
   to "put on the attitude of Jesus,"
   find courage in the fact that
   God is much more patient with you
   than you are with yourself.

God's necessary "surgery on your soul"
  will be healed by the amazing compassion
  of his constant Presence.

But the greatest impact
  of this "fire on the earth,"
  God's most revolutionary challenge,
  lies outside ourselves.
The divine message of the Son of God
  is a refining fire of judgment
  lighting up the passing fixations
    of a self-obsessed culture.
"I have come for division" (Luke 12:51).

Modern culture does not want to change,
  or to be confronted
  with its injustices, denials, and inequities.
Entrenched people will do anything
  to avoid the searing fire of divine division—
  the division of true love from cheap lust,
  of forgiveness and compassion
    from bitterly nursed vengeance,
  of societal "progress"
    from deep, unspoken prejudices.

God's values and commandments
  are a bonfire in the night
  confronting and consuming
  the shallow self-interests
    this world holds so dear.
*"He will baptize you
  in the Holy Spirit and fire"* (Matthew 3:11).

The fiery message of the Spirit of Jesus
  can indeed sear your heart of impurity,
  and refine you to pure gold.

Allow that blinding flame of eternity
to purify your soul,
to cleanse your spirit
of ego-debris and sin,
of passivity and fear.

Then, turn to the world you live in,
and help light a fire for change—
a blazing fire of divine
love, truth, and power.

Salvation Is Free, Not Easy

Twenty-First Sunday in Ordinary Time

(Isaiah 66:18–21; Hebrews 12:5–7, 11–13; Luke 13:22–30)

What is God like?
Children have asked parents
    this question for generations.
The Bible seems at times
    to offer differing answers.
The God portrayed in Isaiah 66:18
    has arms open to welcome
    "nations of every language."
The God portrayed in Luke 13:22
    is a disciplining father
    using "tough love" on people:
    "Enter through the narrow gate."

Which image is correct?
Which view of God
    is more accurate?
Actually, instead of being
        contradictory,
    these two images
        are complementary.
Taken together as one,
    they teach great wisdom.

The kingdom Jesus spoke about
 is not limited
 to a specific "chosen race,"
 any one denomination,
 any special race, creed,
 or group of "super-faithful."
God's home is open
 to all his created children—
 to all who come humbly
  before his presence
 asking for a place in that kingdom,
 living lives that reflect
  a sincere commitment to God.

There will indeed be those in heaven
 whom you did not expect to see!
"I say to you,
 prostitutes and tax collectors
 are entering the Kingdom of God
 before you" (Matthew 21:31).
But then Jesus balances these
 shocking words by adding,
 "Many will attempt to enter
  but be unable."

God's love is free
 but it is not cheap.
God's love is unconditional,
 unbounded and unterritorial—
 but there is a price tag.
The price is personal commitment
 and spiritual discipline.
Awareness of a Higher Power in life
 demands actions that then
 conform one to that Power.

The transforming power of Love
   is released only gradually—
     through ongoing faith
     and dark moments of hope.

The "price" of salvation is paid
   by humble yielding to God,
   transformed attitudes
     toward people,
   faithfulness to regular prayer,
   learned spiritual disciplines,
   willingness to be transformed,
   and increased awareness
     of sin and injustice.
"Lay aside your old way of life,
   and acquire a fresh
   spiritual way of thinking" (Ephesians 4:22).

Because human nature is stubborn,
   and human ego so fixated
     on control and competition,
   true Spirit-seekers know the need
   for constant work
     at spiritual transformation,
     at personal renewal,
     at change of heart.
The salvation and freedom we seek
   is an ongoing process.
"Do not conform yourselves
   to this generation,
   but be transformed
   by the renewal of your mind" (Romans 12:2).

Salvation is indeed free—
   but it is never easy.
One wise writer said it well:
   "Prayer can, indeed, be a torment
   until we are truly transformed
   into what we are saying."

Celebrate the free gift
   of salvation and freedom!
Rejoice in God's love for you,
   in his invitation to eternal peace.
But "enter through the narrow gate";
   beware the pitfalls of ego,
   pride, and self-righteousness.
"Many will come from east and west,
   north and south, to feast
   in the Kingdom of God,"
      but
   "Some who are last will be first,
   and some who are first
   will be last" (Luke 13:29–30).

My Dinner with Jesus

Twenty-Second Sunday in Ordinary Time

(Sirach 3:17–18, 20, 28–29; Luke 14:1, 7–14)

I was invited to dinner last week—
at Rabbi Gamaliel's house.
It was a big event
in my little Israeli town,
and a proud moment for me
(a humble sheep-herder)
to be asked to attend.
Not knowing where to sit,
I took a seat somewhere in the middle
of the long, food-filled table
(next to my friend, Joachim, the carpenter)
and then watched as the village's
"important" people
jockeyed for their places of honor.

I was rather surprised to find
that young Nazarene rabbi,
Jesus Bar-Joseph, there as well.
He preaches all over the countryside,
talking about some "new kingdom"
built on love and forgiveness,
performing, they say, great miracles.

I had never heard him before,
    but now I will never forget him—
    because there is something
        about this teacher—
    something different
        from any other man.
In the one night I watched and listened,
    this young Nazarene prophet taught me—
        a crusty old Jewish tender of sheep—
    more valuable wisdom
    than in all my years
        at the Temple.

Always know your place with God

"Hear O Israel! The Lord is our God!
    He alone shall you adore" (Deuteronomy 6:4).
Rich or poor, beggars or landowners—
    all have a special place
        in God's kingdom,
    a place not determined
        by prestige or status,
    but by the condition of one's soul.
My God has made a place for me;
    have I made a significant place for him
    amidst the clutter of my life?
Is God in the center place of my life?
Do I daily place myself
    in the center of God's will?

The sign of a faith-filled person is humbleness

"Conduct your affairs with humility,
    and you will be loved more
        than a giver of gifts" (Sirach 3:17).

Our God truly loves
   the humbled of heart,
   those who pretend to greatness
     will be brought low.
If I do not choose a simple, childlike attitude toward life,
   I may be forced to it
   by the words or actions of another.
Young Jonas, the self-important tailor,
   learned that lesson that night.
   He was asked to move to a lower place
   when wise old Samuel arrived late.
"Whoever exalts himself
   will be humbled,
whoever humbles himself
   will be exalted" (Luke 14:11).

Generosity to life's broken ones will be repaid in the end

The rabbi Jesus spoke powerfully that night:
   "Give and it will
     be given back to you—
good measure,
   pressed down,
   running over,
will be poured into your garment" (Luke 6:38).
I see now that my life is not complete
   unless I give as freely
     as I have received.
I must not avoid
   the poor and brokenhearted;
   rather, I must reach out
     in kindness and love,
   working to bring God's justice
     to this tired old world.

I pray today that
   I may be worthy of this
   "resurrection of the just"
     that he spoke of—
   but I still have
     so many questions to ask him.
I wonder if he would allow me
   to follow him for a while?
I wonder if he would have
   a place for me?

Abandonment

Twenty-Third Sunday in Ordinary Time

(Philemon 9–10, 12–17; Luke 14:25–33)

Near the city park
　where I used to jog daily,
　there was an abandoned house,
　long empty and boarded up.
As I jogged by I used to wonder
　what kind of stories
　had that building witnessed:
　stories of joy or struggle?
　ecstasy or triumph?
　passion or grief?

There is much abandonment
　in our modern world today—
　a sad cultural byproduct
　of a materialistic society.
Wherever one looks there are
　abandoned houses,
　cars, and junk
　of all sorts.
But truly the worst of all
　are the abandoned people.

Refugees from the horrors of war
   stream out endlessly and mutely
   from play fields
      become killing fields.
Runaway children stare at us
   from milk cartons
   as we eat breakfast.
Homeless people move silently,
   carts full of society's remains,
   modern victims of our urban jungles.
"If a person shuts his ear
   to the cry of the poor,
   he himself will also call
   and not be heard" (Proverbs 21:13).

But abandonment is not just "out there";
   it frequently is much closer
      and more deeply personal—
   a nagging sense of aloneness,
   a persistent sense
      of something missing,
   a lonely isolated feeling
      from an ended relationship,
   a bitter wound of rejection.
Truly we need to hear well
   what our God speaks to us:
"The Lord will not cast off his people
   nor abandon his inheritance" (Psalm 94:14).

The nature of our God is that
   his presence is always greater
   when people struggle the most.
Grace does not depend on feelings,
   certainly not on circumstances around us,
   however horrific they may be.

The prophet Isaiah says it well:
"When you pass through raging waters,
I will be with you.
When you walk through the fire,
you shall not be burned.
Because you are precious in my eyes,
and I love you!" (Isaiah 43:2)

The amazing irony of our God is
 that although the world shunts them aside,
 God actually prefers the abandoned!
Jesus' own friendships and work
 was not with the self-sufficient
 or the satisfied elite of Israel;
 Jesus preferred those who were
  dispossessed,
  downtrodden,
  marginalized.
"People who are healthy
 do not need a doctor,
 sick people do" (Mark 2:17).

Reflect this day on the abandonment
 and ruins of your own life—
 on experiences of exile
  and utter aloneness—
 where you have experienced isolation,
 being cast off or rejected,
 thrown aside and ignored—
 it is there you are most open
  to grace and mercy,
  to God's work of healing.

Become more sensitive and aware
 of the abandoned underclass
 of human beings who cross your path
  every day.

What can you personally do
  to bring a touch of grace—
  the balm of God's presence—
    into their lives?
"Welcome him as you would welcome me" (Philemon 17).

What our modern world abandons,
  God possesses and cherishes.
Where people fail and reject,
  God accepts and blesses.
When all around
  are faithless and false,
  our God remains
  "faithful and true."

The Loving Father

Twenty-Fourth Sunday in Ordinary Time

(Luke 15:1–32)

The younger "prodigal son"?
The "loving father"?
The "self-righteous older son"?

Whatever title you prefer,
   this Bible story
   is one of the world's
      spiritual classics.
There are five stages in the story,
   each a paradigm
   for our journeys as well.

The underlying story theme is *separation*.
The younger son chose separation—
   detaching himself from father,
   family roots, ancestral home.
The older son remained home—
   but was himself "separated"
   by his self-righteous attitudes.

God is always concerned about separation—
    and offers a helping hand
    to anyone experiencing
    the alienation of separation.
"Come to me, all you who labor
    and are heavily burdened . . . " (Matthew 11:28)

After returning, *restoration* occurs—
    the father restores his younger son
    to the fullness
       of his family rights.
Faith is always about the Father
    opening his arms
       without retribution
to welcome the lost back home.
God is always there waiting—
    for anyone who has wandered away.
"This man welcomes sinners
    and eats with them" (Luke 15:2).

After this, a *celebration* has to happen!
God loves to celebrate with his people—
    what else do you think
       heaven will be like!?

Some picture God as an imposing judge
    waiting to censure wayward souls.
    But Jesus reveals a Father
    who can party with the best of us
    when one of his children returns home!
"Rejoice with me because
    I have found my lost sheep!" (Luke 15:6)

Only one person is missing though:
    the self-righteous older son
    who sadly cannot share
       the joy of the moment.

Behind the scenes, there was *cooperation.*
The forgotten people here
   are the household servants—
   the true heroes of Luke 15.
They were satisfied with their "plenty,"
   keeping their eyes faithfully
      upon their Master,
   cooperating fully
      in planning the celebration,
   rejoicing freely
      with the returned son.
"You here are with me always—
   everything I have is yours" (Luke 15:31).

Are you ready to cooperate with God
   as willingly as they?
Or are you stingy with God's grace,
   as was the elder son?
"Give, and it will be given back to you—
   good measure, pressed down, flowing over" (Luke 6:38).

In the end, there is only *consummation*:
   seeing past the narrowness
      of this world
   to fulfillment and freedom
      in the next world.
All our self-important
   human issues and concerns
   will fade away to nothingness
   at "consummation time"—
   the end-times of life.
All that has been separated
   will be restored.
All who have cooperated with God's grace
   will celebrate in perfect peace
      for eternity.

In the end, it matters most
  how we look at life,
  and the depth
    of "divine vision" we have.
God calls us all to look beyond—
  beyond mere human separations and frustrations,
  beyond failure and problems
    to the ultimate purpose of all life.

Keep your eyes on the prize of heaven.
Do not get pulled down "to the pigs"
  by your obsession with this world.
Resist needless separations
  from family, friends, or faith.
Avoid becoming stingy
  with the grace God gives so freely.
When you experience failure or fear,
  know that you can always
  rise up
    and return to your Father.

Speak the Truth in Love

Twenty-Fifth Sunday in Ordinary Time

(1 Timothy 2:1–8; Luke 16:1–13)

In his book *Up From Slavery*,
   Booker Washington speaks of
   a post-slavery itinerant preacher
   wandering throughout the South.
In one town, he was asked by officials
   if he taught that the world
      was flat or round.
The man answered simply,
   "I'm prepared to teach either way,
   depending on who pays my bill!"

This man would likely be popular today—
   far too many in our modern world
   prefer that truth be something
   they can mold, bend, twist, change, and spin
      to their own purposes.
Politicians and pollsters,
   mass media moguls and editors,
   public relations "spin doctors,"
   even some teachers and preachers:

all these fall far too easily
to the deceptive modern temptation
of reshaping reality to one's own liking,
of making truth a relative thing.
*"Truth has stumbled in the streets,
honesty cannot enter"* (Isaiah 59:14).

Truth is not defined by surveys,
popular consensus, or opinion polls.
Truth is not a changeable thing,
malleable or flexible
depending on the situation
we find ourselves in.

Rather, truth flows naturally and intuitively
from inner integrity and honesty,
from adherence to unchanging values.
Truth springs from moral absolutes
rooted deep in our conscience,
taught to us by the God who gave Life.
*"God wants all people to be saved
and come to know the truth"* (1 Timothy 2:4).

Stealing is wrong,
whether by cheating on taxes,
taking another's property,
or shoplifting a candy bar.
Taking a life is an abominable thing,
whether by crime, abortion,
or "killing a good name."
Honesty and integrity is a lifestyle,
not an attribute temporarily donned
to serve our immediate purposes.
Sexuality is a gift of power and procreation,
most appropriately expressed
in permanent commitments
of love and faithfulness.

Honoring God as the primary Truth in life—
    this is the rock that anchors,
    defines, and interprets
    all of these moral absolutes
    in contemporary life situations.
"The truth is this: God is one.
One also is the mediator between God and men,
    the man Christ Jesus" (1 Timothy 2:5).

Seek for eternal truths in your own life.
Do not settle for the empty promises
    that pretend to be modern wisdom.
Find the one whose name is Truth:
    "I am the Way, Truth, and Life."
Go to the Master, Jesus, to ponder
    upon the things of greatest value.

Learn to apply eternal Truths
    to the passing problems of this world.
Turn to wise spiritual people
    for guidance, counsel, and prayer
    in times of confusion or uncertainty.
To act in truth consistently,
    without a second thought,
    spend daily time in prayer
    being nourished and fed
        by words of Truth and Life.

Become a truth-speaker—
    a person who speaks the truth in love.
For, in a world of attractively spun political ideas
    and a "me-first" morality,
    we desperately need men and women
    dedicated to honesty and integrity—
        truth-speakers of love and faith.

*"If you hold to my teaching,
   you really are my disciples.
Then you will know the truth,
   and the truth will set you free"* (John 8:32).

Divine Paradoxes

Twenty-Sixth Sunday in Ordinary Time

(Amos 6:1, 4–7; Luke 16:19–31)

The word "paradox" is defined
as "something opposite in meaning
to what is expected."
According to this definition,
our God seems to love paradoxes;
they are at the heart
of most of what God has told us.

Jesus often used conflicting images
to challenge and confront us:
"The last shall be first,
the first shall be last."
"The meek shall inherit the earth."
"The greatest in God's kingdom
will be the least."

Many people in the Bible
had life-converting experiences
revolving around events or moments
that were highly paradoxical.

A powerful politician named Nicodemus,
  known and renowned publicly,
  had to sneak by night to visit Jesus.
Once a nameless prostitute
  came to believe in Jesus,
  while a wealthy man Jesus was visiting
    did not.
The cocky Simon Peter was humbled
  by Jesus consistently
  before being named "the rock."

When we follow God seriously,
  we must allow the Lord
  to turn us upside down as well.
The first thing God often does
  when we begin to seriously follow him
  is extremely paradoxical;
  God may upset the control, balance, and order
  many of us have striven so vigorously to establish.
"Do you think I have come for peace?
  I assure you the contrary is true:
  I have come for division" (Luke 12:51).

The prophet Amos cries out wisdom
  in words that shock today's world:
  "Woe to the complacent!" (Amos 6:1)

Watch out for becoming
  too self-satisfied and secure,
  too overly comfortable and cozy,
  too totally "in control"
    of every aspect of your life.
The very core of God's message
  is exactly the opposite:
  "Let go! Give up control!"
  "Into your hands
    I commend my spirit!"

God's paradoxical divine wisdom
    may seem enigmatic and mysterious.
But remember that the God for whom
    "a thousand years are as a day"
    has wisdom far vaster and wiser than ours.
God does not judge the way we do—
    "God's ways are not our ways" (Isaiah 55:8).

The events happening in the Gospel today
    mirror these truths.
The rich man who daily feasted splendidly
    eventually suffered for eternity,
    while the long-suffering Lazarus
    "was carried by angels
        to Abraham's bosom."

Jesus can indeed set you free,
    give eternal happiness,
    deep inner healing—
    but more often than not,
    he may make you miserable first!
God may have to turn you upside first
    before his peace can rest in your heart.

Become familiar with the paradoxes of God,
    and learn to love
    the mysterious ways God works.

Give up controlling attitudes—
    and gain peace
    that passes understanding.

Seek first the values of God's Kingdom—
    and discover unforeseen
    earthly blessings.

To find true life and happiness—
   lose your life in God and service.
To be great and important—
   become a servant to others.
To inherit the greatest wealth of all—
   become humble, gentle, compassionate.

Increase Our Faith?

Twenty-Seventh Sunday in Ordinary Time

(2 Timothy 1:6–8,13–14; Luke 17:5–10)

We are obsessed today with having "more":
more money than we already have,
more time to do more things,
more space in our homes,
more success in our life.
We even carry this over to God,
desiring more peace,
more faith,
more patience,
more time to pray,
more of God in our life.

It seems we have a major problem
in this modern, most prosperous of times,
being satisfied
with what we already have.
The important question of this day
is not
"How do I get more?",
but rather,
"How much is enough?"

Just what does it take to fully sate
　　this unending, obsessive human desire
　　to accumulate and amass
　　far beyond what is truly needed?

When God is active in our life,
　　divinely ordered priorities predominate;
　　and the real question becomes—
　　not "Do I need more?" but
　　　"Have I used what God
　　　has already given me?"
God's Spirit, already made present
　　when we experienced
　　　the waters of rebirth,
　　is sufficient for the tasks at hand.

The apostles today ask Jesus,
　　"Increase our faith."
The response he gives is profound.
"If you had faith
　　the size of a mustard seed,
　　you could say to the mulberry tree,
　　'Be uprooted and planted in the sea,'
　　and it would obey you" (Luke 17:6).

In other words, Jesus is saying,
　　"Don't ask me for *more* faith—
　　use and release the faith you have!
　　The Spirit present within you
　　　is enough!
　　Start relying totally on me.
　　Trust me so completely
　　　in all things,
　　and you will even make
　　　trees and mountains move!"

Divine "faith" is much misunderstood.
It is not measured
    the way the world measures:
    with limits, amounts, and dimensions.
We never "use up" or "run out of" faith;
    faith is not a quantifiable entity,
    but a living Reality in the soul.

Faith is a divine Presence
    roaming about in the depths
        of our being.
Faith is that infinite Power within,
    always available
        for the needs at hand.
Faith is that mysterious Wisdom beyond logic,
    giving direction, purpose, and meaning
        to life.

The task of true spirituality
    is not so much the increasing of faith,
    as it is the releasing of faith—
    the unleashing of that awesome Energy
        already present within us;
    the penetrating of that Wisdom
        our God has already gifted us with.

"Stir into flame
    the gift God bestowed . . .
    the Spirit God gave
    is no cowardly spirit,
    but one that makes you
        strong, wise and loving.
Never be ashamed
    of your testimony
        for our Lord" (2 Timothy 1:6–8).

Step out in the faith
  you already have.
Release the faith-filling Spirit of God
  lying dormant within.
Worship in churches, pray with people
  truly empowered with faith
  and alive in the Spirit of God—
  that you may learn to unleash
  the Power of faith within.
Live life with open hands of trust
  rather than closed fists of control.
Let go of "accumulating" and "increasing";
  let go in the empowering Faith
  of the God within!

Disease and Grace

Twenty-Eighth Sunday in Ordinary Time

(2 Kings 5:14–17; Luke 17:11–19)

The dreaded diseases of today
    are cancer and AIDS.
There is no cure yet for either—
    both are deadly,
    both are feared and fearsome.
The dreaded disease of Jesus' day
    was leprosy.
A twenty-five-hunrdred-year-old scourge,
    it was permanently deforming
    and horribly contagious.
People who contracted leprosy
    were shunned and condemned
        to isolation.

Yet twice today God takes on
    the disease of leprosy—
    with healing and wholeness
        as a result!
Namaan is cured
    by plunging into a river;
    and ten lepers cured
        on the road to the Temple.

The lesson here is this:
   God has power
      where human power fails!
"For man it is impossible
   but not for God.
   With God all things
      are possible" (Mark 10:27).

Such horrible diseases
   have always been feared
   because once contracted,
   we have little human control.
To a great extent,
   we are simply powerless—
   and this perhaps
   is the greatest human fear.
When we are without
   viable options,
   with little control
      in an overwhelming situation,
   the human spirit is shaken
   and severely challenged.

Actually, it is a complete illusion
   to believe that we
   can control reality or people.
Cancer, AIDS, addictions, human weaknesses:
   these are only a few things
   human willpower
      can never truly control.
True spirituality begins
   with an essential revelation:
   when we are powerless,
      it is then that we have Power!
"My grace is enough for you,
   for my power
   is made perfect
      in your weakness" (2 Corinthians 12:9).

The only way to find inner peace,
　　to be "saved" in the face of
　　　　overwhelming disease or problems,
　　is by yielding to a Higher Power—
　　　　the Power of God and Life.
The men in Scripture today
　　found healing
　　　　only after turning to God
　　　　in their powerlessness—
　　admitting their utter neediness,
　　yielding up everything
　　　　to that Higher Power.
Peter said it well:
　　"Lord, where can we go?
　　You have the words
　　　　of eternal life" (John 6:68).

Faith is never as much
　　about "controlling"
　　　　(doing, disciplining, even believing)
　　as it is about trusting
　　　　(releasing, yielding, and letting go).
The hardest thing
　　we will do in life
　　is not dealing with
　　　　a horrible disease,
　　　　or enduring terrible trials;
　　it is finding Peace
　　　　in powerlessness.
It is letting go of attempts
　　to control God and the world.
It is yielding a stubborn human ego
　　to that Power surpassing understanding,
　　to that ageless wise Spirit,
　　to that most gentle, gracious Being
　　　　called God.

Our wounded, dis-eased spirits
   are made whole
   not by the ego's
      control or scheming,
   nor by self-righteous
      venting of anger,
but by humbly "coming to the waters"
   of cleansing Life,
   by gently "presenting ourselves
      to the priests."

Healing is found in complete yielding
   of ourselves to God.
It is an attitude of
   trust in times of turmoil,
   peace in times of powerlessness.
It is gratitude for the healing Life
   we already have
   in the Presence within us
      of true Power.

WEEK 49

Persistence

Twenty-Ninth Sunday in Ordinary Time

(Exodus 17:8–13; 2 Timothy 3:14–4:2; Luke 18:1–8)

Jules Verne is considered
    the pioneer of science fiction.
He authored truly classic works
    that have become legendary.
But you may not know that at age twenty-five,
    he was rejected by fourteen publishers
    before finding one
    that would accept
    his first completed manuscript,
    20,000 Leagues
    Under the Sea.
Persistence pays off.
This is a divine lesson
    as well as a valuable human one.
The greatest successes in the world
    have rarely come except with a price
    of immense patience and perseverance.
"Stay with the task,
    whether convenient or inconvenient,
    never losing patience" (2 Timothy 4:2).

Moses won a great victory
   over the Amalekite army
   when he (with a little help)
   persisted in holding his hands
   upraised in prayer until sunset.
Jesus used stories to teach
   the "necessity of praying always,
   and never losing heart."
The poor widow of Luke 18
   won her eventual victory
   by her stubborn, persistent knocking
     on that poor judge's door.

The great Walt Disney
   went bankrupt seven times
   before he found success.
The legendary Babe Ruth
   struck out far more times
   (setting a major league record)
   than the 714 home runs he hit.
The inventor Alexander Graham Bell
   failed consistently
   in developing a hearing aid
   for his deaf wife—
   yet eventually stumbled into something
   we now call a "telephone."

When we were brought into this world,
   there was no lifetime warranty given
   protecting us from problems or stress.
God has never promised anyone
   in any time or generation,
   that life in this temporary home
     would be easy,
     without troubles,
     without pain,
     without struggle.

God has made one promise, however,
    that he has never failed to keep:
    he is with us always,
    and gifts us with all we need.
"Know that I am with you always,
    until the end of the world" (Matthew 28:20).

The inborn gifts of our spirit,
    placed dormant within us by God,
    await only the seeds of struggle
        to be brought to life.
Problems challenge our gifts
    into the fullness of life.
Struggles stretch our inner spirit
    to new levels of creativity,
    unlocking doorways to unknown resources.
Patience and persistence are the keys
    unleashing the power
    behind those doors.

Your greatest inner resource—
    the depth and power of faith—
    can never blossom to flower
    without the stress and strain,
    the grief and grind,
        of life-challenges.
In the same way that a caterpillar
    cannot become a butterfly
        without straining against its cocoon,
so, too, your greatest life-progress
    will be made rubbing up against
        the polishing stone of struggles.

You grow in faith and gifts
    by daily prayer and honest work.
But you make light-speed progress
    by patient persistence in struggles.

Continue to believe
   in times of testing.
Persist in praying
   in times of trial.
Persevere in acts of integrity
   in times of trouble.
Always trust in God,
   and know God trusts you.
"Stay with the task,
   whether convenient or inconvenient,
   never losing patience!" (2 Timothy 4:2)

Right with Self or Right with God?

Thirtieth Sunday in Ordinary Time

(2 Timothy 4:6–8, 16–18; Luke 18:9–14)

The difference between
   a laser and a lightbulb
   is simply a matter of focus.
A lightbulb emits scattered light,
   whereas a laser beam of light
   is intensely focused and concentrated.

This same issue of focus
   happens to be the key
   for people seeking the Spirit.
Many people pray today,
   many meditate and read,
   even worship regularly—
   but where is their central focus?
What is the core concern,
   the focused passion of the heart
   underlying their external actions?

The Pharisee in Luke 18
   was focused on doing
   the ritually correct thing:

---

having the traditional posture,
the right words,
the proper dress.
But the central focus of his prayer
was wrongly placed;
he contrasts his own prayer
with the prayer of another.
The focus is not on God but on self—
on cataloguing his own achievements,
boasting of his own orthodoxy.
His sin is self-righteousness
and self-absorption.
"Everyone who exalts himself
shall be humbled" (Luke 18:14).

How much of our spirituality,
our prayers, and spirit-seeking,
is absorbed with meeting our own needs,
solving our own problems,
capturing good "feelings"
about life, self, God?
The spiritual journey is not about
our own personal fulfillment;
this is a twenty-first-century obsession,
but has never been the core focus
of history's true Spirit-seekers.

The tax collector in Luke 18
was externally of lower class,
less social status.
He, too, used the traditional
Jewish prayer posture and style.
Yet his approach to God
is entirely different;
there is no thought of self-value,
no focus on personal accomplishments,
desired achievements,
or merited blessings.

His prayer is sincerely outer-focused;
    there is immense self-honesty,
    deep humbleness and simplicity,
    true inner integrity.
"Oh God, be merciful
    to me a sinner" (Luke 18:13).

His awareness is outside himself;
    although conscious of human frailty,
    his spiritual center has shifted
    from the human mind
        to the divine Mind.
His walk with God is properly focused:
    aware but accepting of human smallness,
    cognizant of inner tensions
    yet utterly God-reliant and trusting.

"This man went home from the temple
    justified"—right with God—
    while the other left
        self-justified,
        self-righteous,
        self-obsessed.

For many today,
    being right with self
        is more important
    than becoming right with God.
The modern focus is self-fulfillment:
    "Do whatever you want,
    as long as you are happy."
The moral compass of the modern conscience
    centers inevitably on self—
    with tragic, terrible consequences.
"Whoever humbles himself
    shall be exalted."

The focus that frees the human spirit
   lies beyond this existence—
   in being right with God alone.
How others act and respond to God
   then becomes irrelevant.
Pain, struggle, and loss are transformed
   into something bigger than self.
Strength becomes weakness,
   failure becomes success—
   because our focus is not
      on what is seen
      but unseen.
"Whoever loses his life for me
   will save it."

Who are you right with?
What is the true focus
   of your prayer and seeking:
   self-justification
   or God's sometimes searing wisdom?
"To God be glory
   forever and ever. Amen" (2 Timothy 4:18).

Sin Has a Tail

Thirty-First Sunday in Ordinary Time

(Wisdom 11:22–12:1; Luke 19:1–10)

While fishing in Canada years ago,
   I was casting rather hastily
   and several times
   badly snarled my line.
While unraveling the fishing line
   one of those innumerable times,
   an insight dawned on me:
   something done in a second
   can take hours to undo.

Sin can be like that;
   indeed it has a long tail.
What is done quickly and carelessly
   in moments of passion,
      lust, or greed,
   often has far-reaching implications.
A frenzied moment of sexual excitement
   can result in new life conceived,
   disease transmitted,
      commitments made.

Words spoken in angered response
   can result in decades of hurt,
   bitter resentments, walls of isolation.

"Punishment [is inflicted]
   for the father's sins
   on children to the
      third and fourth generation;
   but mercy bestowed down
      to the thousandth generation
   on the children of those who love me
      and keep my commandments" (Exodus 20:5–6).

Since sin has a long tail,
   actions of forgiveness
      need one as well.
Admitting our mistakes
   is the first step—
   but only the bare minimum required
   to be touched
      by God's compassion.
"I acknowledge my offense,
   my sin is before me always" (Psalm 51:5).

Those who walk deeply with God
   know that
   although forgiveness is free
      (it cannot be earned or merited),
   it demands an ongoing response
   and has a definite price.
The response demanded
   is acting upon the forgiveness
   we so freely received.

The standard for true spirit-seekers is not
   "What does the law require me to do?"
      but rather
   "What does Christian love require?"

God went far beyond the minimum required
   when he died on the cross for us.
Zacchaeus today went far beyond
   the price God required for forgiveness,
   making up financially and personally
   for all his actions had done.

The price of forgiveness is restitution:
   doing things to help make up
   for any damage or hurt
     our failure has caused.
The price of forgiveness is gratitude:
   expressing praise
   by our prayers and words
     for God's amazing actions
     in our life.
The price of forgiveness is humble contriteness:
   confessing sinfulness nightly,
   being aware how little things
     innocently done
     can affect so many others.

Sin indeed has a long tail.
Thankfully for us,
   divine forgiveness
   also has a long reach.
"Zacchaeus, hurry down.
   I mean to stay
     at your house today" (Luke 19:5).
Become as eager to walk daily
   in God's compassion and mercy,
   as was Zacchaeus to climb a tree
     to see his Master.

The gift of forgiveness
   is freely given
     to the humble of heart.

However, be willing to pay the price
of awareness, surrender, gratitude:
awareness of humble dependency,
surrender to God's transforming power,
gratitude for the gift of mercy.
"Today salvation has come
to this house,
for this is what it means
to be a son of Abraham" (Luke 19:10).

ᵗℏᵉ State of ᵞour Soul

Thirty-Third Sunday in Ordinary Time

(2 Maccabees 7:1–2, 8–14; Luke 20:27–38)

We live in a body-centered culture.
Health clubs are jammed with people
   dedicated to bodily perfection.
Un-nameable devices
   in innumerable health clubs
   are dedicated
   to keeping the body "in shape."
Careers have been made
   and subcultures created
   around diets,
     healthy eating,
     thigh-masters.
Modern media and mass advertising
   obsess about youthful "sexiness,"
   selling everything imaginable
   with "beautiful people."

It is good to be concerned
   about physical health;

this is a key part
of holistic spirituality,
of the body-soul-mind transformation
   God brings.
Paul says *"Did you not know*
  that your body
  is a temple of the Holy Spirit?" (Romans 6:19)

But complete health
  and total well-being
  demands moving beyond
    care of the physical body;
  it means serious concern
  with our spiritual body,
  with the state
    of our immortal soul.

How healthy and alive
  is your soul—
  that eternal part
    of your truest Self,
  which is Guide,
    conscience, and Spirit?
What is the condition
  of your inner Spirit?

Upon this question hangs the choice
  of your eternal resting place.
"What good will it be for a person
  if he gains the whole world,
  but forfeits his soul?" (Matthew 16:26)

In Maccabees, four brothers
  give up their bodies
  for a greater good
    than this world—
  for the eternal soul-values
    of their God.

"It was from heaven
I received these hands;
for God's laws I disdain them;
from him I hope to receive
them again" (2 Maccabees 7:11).
Looking beyond their physical bodies,
   they discovered true "soul-health"—
the eternal Life and health
   of heaven.

Jesus dealt with total body health,
   answering tough questions
      about our physical bodies.
In essence, he said,
   "You've got it all wrong!
   The physical doesn't matter!
      Your spiritual relationships
      are what make the difference."
"Do not be afraid
   of those who kill the body
      but cannot kill the soul.
   Rather, be afraid of the One
   who can destroy
      both body and soul
      in hell" (Matthew 10:28).

What is the state of your immortal soul?
Take care of your physical body:
   watch what you eat,
      exercise regularly;
   but do not neglect the health
      of your spiritual body.

Are you taking time for daily prayer,
   for meditation, and quiet?
What is the last spiritual book you read?

Do you know where your Bible is,
   and do you read
     God's "love-letter" often?
What is the status
   of your friendship with Jesus?
   Personal and intimate,
     or distant and detached?

Do your attitude and actions with people
   reveal a gentle, patient,
     understanding spirit?
Is your emotional world
   in balance and harmony—
   without resentment, bitterness,
     anger, or fear
     polluting your spirit?
What actions do you undertake in justice
   for the improvement of our world?

These questions
   are "health-checks" for the soul.
Faith in the physical body alone
   is fragile—
   lasting only as long
     as we are healthy.
It is when we are
   resurrected from the body
     and our fixation upon it
   that we truly triumph
     and live eternally.

Apocalypse—Now?

Thirty-Third Sunday in Ordinary Time

(Malachi 3:19–20; Luke 21:5–19)

It is a horrible thing
    when a world comes to an end.
Placid villages ravaged
    by warfare;
peaceful people seized
    into slavery;
students shot to death
    in a high school massacre;
sudden and unexpected deaths
    of loved ones:
these remind us of the fragility
    of our little worlds.

Scripture today speaks of life's "end-times"
    with cryptic words like
        "the day that is coming
        will set them on fire,"
and dreadful descriptions like
    "There will be earthquakes, famines . . .
        and in the sky
        fearsome omens and great signs" (Luke 21:11).

But "end-times" have touched us all.
Perhaps once your own world "fell apart";
    perhaps even now you walk through
    dark "apocalyptic" moments.
Certainly and inevitably
    your own private "end-time"
    will one day occur.

Our God offers wisdom for those
    "end-times" moments of our lives.
"Stay awake! You do not know
    the day nor the hour" (Matthew 25:13).
Live life with brutal honesty
    yet bold faith—
    be always ready to meet your Creator.

"Do not worry . . .
    I will give you words and wisdom" (Luke 21:16).
Do not live in denial or fear
    of that "great and terrible day"
    that will one day touch you.
The Spirit's Presence will be
    your anchor in this world,
    your guarantee in the next.

"Take care not to be misled . . .
    many will come claiming 'I am he' . . .
    do not follow them" (Luke 21:8).
God alone
    has what the human heart looks for.
Beware of shallow mass-media charlatans
    or superficial "feel-good" wisdom.

When worlds are falling apart,
    one needs to hold
        to unchanging things:
    to eternal verities and proven Powers.

Keep your eyes on the Master;
    he "has the words of eternal life."
Build your spiritual house now
    on the rock of God's strength
    rather than the sand
        of worldly treasure.

"Not a hair of your head
    will be harmed.
By patient endurance
    you will be saved" (Luke 21:17).
This is God's personal word to you—
    a promise made
        for all ages and endings,
    a promise to meditate on
        and rely upon.
"You will be saved."
This does not mean
    that you will have
        no struggles or sufferings in life
        or that "end-times"
        will never occur.
It means that your human spirit,
    when depending on the divine Spirit,
    cannot be harmed when worlds *do*
        come crashing down—
    for *"greater is he that is in you*
        than he that is in the world" (1 John 4:4).

By patient endurance,
    Jesus himself walked
        through an "end-time"—
    all the way to Calvary's cross
        and beyond—
    to new Life, healing, hope, and joy.

By patient endurance and trust,
   you, too, can walk
     the "end-times roads"
  of loss, pain, and death—
  all the way
     to renewed vision, strength, trust.
For your God-Friend has told you
   "I go before you always."

Worlds will come to an end.
Awful apocalypses will appear,
   and endings will occur often
     in your life
     and in the lives others.
But *"for those who fear my name,*
   there will arise the Sun of justice
   with its healing rays" (Malachi 3:20).

King and Lord

Christ the King

(Colossians 1:12–20; Luke 23:35–43)

Kings, lords, and princes:
    Americans have little understanding
    of these "foreign" concepts.
These terms are more familiar
    in other countries,
    to more formal cultures,
    like England and Japan.

To pragmatic American "common" eyes,
    the concept of our God
    as a "King" or "Lord"
    seems distant and aloof,
    unnaturally formal and foreign.
But our American disdain
    for these symbolic images
    may well be a great loss.

Great archetypal truths
    are captured in the concept
    of a royal and regal figure,
    a powerful yet wise leader
    of millions of people.

"You are the king of kings . . .
to you the God in heaven has given
dominion and strength,
power and glory . . . " (Daniel 2:37)

A *king* is simply one
who has great powers of leadership,
as well as authority,
wisdom, and respect
for people uniquely bound to him.
Is not Jesus Christ of Nazareth
the greatest leader
this world has ever seen?
Does he not have a unique authority
which is life-giving,
empowering, and encouraging?
Does this Leader not deserve
our utmost respect,
our deepest love,
our infinite gratitude?

Are we not particularly bound
to this most amazing King—
a man who gave his very life
that the people he loved and served
might live forever?
"There was an inscription over his head,
'This is the King of the Jews.'"
Jesus is indeed a *king*
for our world today,
for endless ages.
"It is he who is the head
of the body, the Church;
he who is the beginning . . .
that primacy may be his
in everything" (Colossians. 1:18).

A *lord* is simply one
   who has dominion and power,
   authority yet concern
   for people under his care.
Does not Jesus Christ of Nazareth
   have dominion and power
   over every created being,
   every living object
   in a world he helped create?
Does not the power of his Spirit
   flow through and in you
   each and every day,
   gifting you for life's challenges
   beyond your knowledge?
Is not this God-Man Jesus Christ
   concerned for each individual person
   who is struggling or searching,
   lonely or lost?

Whatever term you use for your God,
   give praise and worship daily
   to the One
   who gave his life for you.
Order your life properly,
   making sure that
   "he is before all else that is" (Colossians 1:17).

At the beginning of each day,
   honor the King
     who is "the image of the invisible God,"
   the Lord "through whom we have redemption,
     the forgiveness of our sins."
Pray with humble simplicity
   the words of the thief on the cross:
   "Lord, remember me
   when you enter your kingdom" (Luke 23:42).

Praise the powerful One
   "whose name
   is above all other names."
Give glory to One
   who is the gentle Lamb of God,
   the Prince of Peace,
      the King of Kings, Lord of Lords!

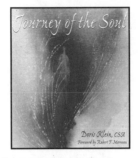

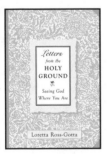